PEOPLE
IN THE **NEWS**

Arnold Schwarzenegger

by Karen Brandon

LUCENT
BOOKS ®

THOMSON
———— ✳ ———— ™
GALE

San Diego • Detroit • New York • San Francisco • Cleveland
New Haven, Conn. • Waterville, Maine • London • Munich

THOMSON
GALE

Titles in the People in the News series include:

Adam Sandler
Ben Affleck
Bill Gates
Bono
Britney Spears
Christopher Reeve
Colin Powell
Elijah Wood
Eminem
George W. Bush
Jennifer Lopez
Jennifer Love Hewitt
Jesse Jackson
Jim Carrey
J.K. Rowling
Johnny Depp
Julia Roberts

Mel Gibson
Michael Jackson
Michael J. Fox
Nicholas Cage
Oprah Winfrey
The Osbournes
Princess Diana
Prince William
Reese Witherspoon
R.L. Stine
Robin Williams
Sandra Bullock
Steven Spielberg
Tiger Woods
Tom Cruise
Tony Blair
Will Smith

LIBRARY OF CONGRESS CATALOGING-IN-PUBLICATION DATA

Brandon, Karen.
  Arnold Schwarzenegger / by Karen Brandon.
    p. cm. —— (People in the news)
Includes bibliographical references and index.
Contents: Big dreams in a small town—The Austrian Oak—Going Hollywood—
Marrying into American royalty—Governor Schwarzenegger.
  ISBN 1-59018-539-0
1. Schwarzenegger, Arnold—Juvenile literature. 2. Motion picture actors and
actresses—United States—Biography—Juvenile literature. 3. Bodybuilders—United
States—Biography—Juvenile literature. 4. Governors—California—Biography—
Juvenile literature. [1. Schwarzenegger, Arnold. 2. Actors and actresses. 3. Body-
builders. 4. Governors.] I. Title. II. Series: People in the news (San Diego, Calif.)
PN2287.S3368B73 2004
791.4302'8'092—dc22
                                                                    2003026221

jBiography
Schwarzenegger

Table of Contents

Foreword

F<small>AME AND CELEBRITY</small> are alluring. People are drawn to those who walk in fame's spotlight, whether they are known for great accomplishments or for notorious deeds. The lives of the famous pique public interest and attract attention, perhaps because their experiences seem in some ways so different from, yet in other ways so similar to, our own.

Newspapers, magazines, and television regularly capitalize on this fascination with celebrity by running profiles of famous people. For example, television programs such as *Entertainment Tonight* devote all of their programming to stories about entertainment and entertainers. Magazines such as *People* fill their pages with stories of the private lives of famous people. Even newspapers, newsmagazines, and television news frequently delve into the lives of well-known personalities. Despite the number of articles and programs, few provide more than a superficial glimpse at their subjects.

Lucent's People in the News series offers young readers a deeper look into the lives of today's newsmakers, the influences that have shaped them, and the impact they have had in their fields of endeavor and on other people's lives. The subjects of the series hail from many disciplines and walks of life. They include authors, musicians, athletes, political leaders, entertainers, entrepreneurs, and others who have made a mark on modern life and who, in many cases, will continue to do so for years to come.

These biographies are more than factual chronicles. Each book emphasizes the contributions, accomplishments, or deeds that have brought fame or notoriety to the individual and shows how that person has influenced modern life. Authors portray their subjects in a realistic, unsentimental light. For example, Bill Gates—the cofounder and chief executive officer of the software giant Microsoft—has been instrumental in making personal computers the most vital tool of the modern age. Few dispute his business savvy, his perseverance, or his technical expertise, yet critics say he is ruthless in his dealings with competitors and driven more by his desire to maintain Microsoft's dominance in the computer industry than by an interest in furthering technology.

In these books, young readers will encounter inspiring stories about real people who achieved success despite enormous obstacles. Oprah Winfrey—the most powerful, most watched, and wealthiest woman on television today—spent the first six years of her life in the care of her grandparents while her unwed mother sought work and a better life elsewhere. Her adolescence was colored by promiscuity, pregnancy at age fourteen, rape, and sexual abuse.

Each author documents and supports his or her work with an array of primary and secondary source quotations taken from diaries, letters, speeches, and interviews. All quotes are footnoted to show readers exactly how and where biographers derive their information and provide guidance for further research. The quotations enliven the text by giving readers eyewitness views of the life and accomplishments of each person covered in the People in the News series.

In addition, each book in the series includes photographs, annotated bibliographies, timelines, and comprehensive indexes. For both the casual reader and the student researcher, the People in the News series offers insight into the lives of today's newsmakers—people who shape the way we live, work, and play in the modern age.

Introduction

The Master of Reinvention

IN 1977, THE year the movie *Pumping Iron* was released, the *Soho Weekly News* published a front-page story characterizing the movie's star, Arnold Schwarzenegger, as a fleeting sensation destined to fade. At the time, the New York City newspaper was regarded as an arbiter of everything hip, but events soon underscored the extent of its miscalculation on Schwarzenegger. After dismissing him as a passing fancy, the *Soho Weekly News* folded, while Arnold Schwarzenegger proceeded on a course toward a meteoric ascent.

Arnold Schwarzenegger could be considered America's ultimate master of reinvention. It is impossible to think of any other modern figure who has scaled the heights of such diverse pursuits—sports, movies, and politics. His conquests have made him one of the most unique figures on the American landscape —a symbol of self improvement, a subject of cartoonish impersonation and satire, an action figure hero whose violence saves humankind, and an extraordinary symbol of immigrant success in America.

Of course, many others before him straddled some of the same spheres. Other athletes—among them the bodybuilder Reg Parks and swimmer Johnny Weissmuller, who were Schwarzenegger's boyhood heroes—turned to acting. Other sports figures—such as Muhammad Ali—transcended athletics to become symbols of an American era. Other actors—most prominently President Ronald Reagan, whose bust Schwarzenegger displays in his office—found success on the national political stage.

Still, none of these predecessors matches Schwarzenegger's success in so many pursuits at such stratospheric levels. Though he chose a sport that was the laughingstock of athletics, Schwarzenegger's bodybuilding career transformed the sport itself, turning the pursuit of a better body into something of a national passion. Though his signature movies were derided for their violence and never won acclaim for their artistic merit, they became the blockbusters of their day. Though his physique, accent, and wooden acting style were viewed as insurmountable impediments to Hollywood success, they became Schwarzenegger hallmarks. Those endlessly caricatured traits established Schwarzenegger as an icon of pop culture. His long name became a household word. His Bavarian accent and monotone delivery proved irresistible fodder for thousands of imitators. His movie

Arnold Schwarzenegger has enjoyed success as a bodybuilder, as an actor, and, most recently, as a politician. Here, he gives a thumbs-up after being sworn in as governor of California on November 17, 2003.

lines established themselves as fixtures in the pop lexicon of the day. And then, in a single leap, Schwarzenegger landed in the most prominent political office in the land for which he was eligible—governor of California.

Yet as diverse as these unlikely occupations seem, the roles —Mr. Universe, Mr. Action Hero, and Mr. Governor—are linked in unlikely ways. They all are the result of a single image, that of physical power. Schwarzenegger's determined exploitation of his defined and defining muscles lies beneath all of his successes. It led to his conquest of bodybuilding, to the larger-than-life roles in the movies, and, as a result, to the can-do, take-charge image that played a role in his political success. All these accomplishments seem to stem from a single skill: salesmanship. On the morning after the 2003 election, the *Los Angeles Times* observed of the state's governor-elect,

> His life, as he has told it in interviews and books over the last 25 years, is the story of a man who could sell anything—and has. He has sold T-shirts, tank tops, weight-lifting belts, gym bags, exercise videos, weights, bricklaying services, bodybuilding for women, magazines, bicycles, motorcycles, Hummers, books, seminars, movies, German food, cigars, restaurants, real estate, malls, sports for inner-city children, after-school programs, [the noted economist] Milton Friedman, Austria, the English language, the United States—and above all, self improvement.[1]

Schwarzenegger's accomplishments were no accident. They were shrewdly calculated pursuits, the product of the man's unbridled ambition, love of center stage, and yearning for power—even immortality. He reveled in flouting the assumptions of the day—that a muscleman could not be smart; that a Hollywood star could not make it with a thick accent; that an actor with a scant public résumé could not appear in movies and, at the same time, begin a political career in a high-profile elective office.

Schwarzenegger shaped his destiny as clearly and deliberately as he shaped his body, and the result is a life that quite resembles his famed deltoids and calves—improbable, outlandish, and outsized.

Chapter 1

Big Dreams in a Small Town

ARNOLD ALOIS SCHWARZENEGGER was born in the predawn hours of July 30, 1947, in Thal, a tiny village tucked into the picturesque hills and forests of the Austrian countryside. His birth came one year after the birth of his brother, Meinhard, and two years after the end of World War II. His father, Gustav Schwarzenegger, worked as a police chief in the farming and lumber town of some twelve hundred residents, and his mother, Aurelia Jadrny, who had been widowed in a previous marriage, was a traditional homemaker.

The couple had married on October 20, 1945, just weeks after the end of World War II, when Gustav Schwarzenegger was thirty-eight, fifteen years older than his bride.

The Schwarzenegger family, like many families throughout Europe, struggled during those austere postwar years. They lived on the second floor of a three-hundred-year-old house that came with Gustav Schwarzenegger's position as police chief. The house had no indoor plumbing, no central heating system, and for many years, no refrigerator—typical of the standards of the day throughout much of postwar Europe. The Schwarzenegger boys shared a room that had a window overlooking an old castle. They were expected to rise early in the morning to do chores—split and stack wood, haul coal for the stove, and carry well water to the house—in order to "earn" their breakfasts before going to school in a two-room schoolhouse. The family economized by eating meat only once a week.

Arnold Schwarzenegger's Origins

Arnold's Schwarzenegger grew up in Thal, a small town in the foothills of the magnificent Austrian Alps, pictured here.

Arnold Schwarzenegger has boasted that he had the best mother anyone could have had. Aurelia Schwarzenegger made her family and her home her life's work. "She designed the daily routine for my brother and me, let us know when we could play, when we had to study," Schwarzenegger says. "She took care of the cleanliness of the house, and she was a fanatic. You could eat off the floors. The towels would have sharp corners when they were folded and stacked up."[2]

A Demanding Father

With his slicked-back hair and razor-thin mustache, the tall and witty Gustav Schwarzenegger cut a debonair figure, so much so that he was once described as an "Austrian Cary Grant,"[3] a reference to a dashing Hollywood leading man of the day. He was an accomplished musician—playing six instruments and directing the local police band—and a skilled athlete, at one time an amateur champion in the ice sport of curling. Charming as Gustav Schwarzenegger could be, however, he could also burst into fits of rage, many of them lubricated by drink. "There was never enough money, never enough food on the table," one Arnold Schwarzenegger biographer, Robert Lipsyte, writes. "Sometimes Gustav got violent, screaming and thrashing through the house, his temper soaked in alcohol."[4]

Gustav Schwarzenegger bore a dark wartime past, the details of which remain largely shrouded in mystery even today. The elder Schwarzenegger was a member of the Nazi Party, a subject his son and his wife would later insist the family never broached. The silence was said to be commonplace among many Austrian families. "In those days you didn't ask your father," explains Werner Kopacka, a Graz journalist who befriended Schwarzenegger in the 1980s. "None of us talked much about the war."[5]

Indeed, in the Austria of Schwarzenegger's youth, a "culture of denial" thrived for many years after the war. "Austrians lagged well behind the Germans in acknowledging their role in the war and in the persecution of Jews," writes a *Los Angeles Times* correspondent who traveled to Thal to examine Schwarzenegger's roots. "The country of (Adolf) Hitler's birth preferred to think of itself as the Nazi leader's first victim, not his enthusiastic accomplice."[6]

Long after the war Gustav Schwarzenegger retained a love of the military's discipline and regimentation. He applied his strict, military-like philosophy to the upbringing of his sons and the tenor of his role as the head of the family. Arnold Schwarzenegger later said his father ran the family as if he were its general.

Two Different Brothers

The two Schwarzenegger boys were a study in contrasts. Meinhard was charismatic, handsome, and blond. Arnold was timid, darker, with large ears and, for a time, thick glasses. Meinhard was treated as the family's favored son to such a degree that a family friend, noticing the discrepancy in the way the two were treated, dubbed the younger boy, "Cinderella." Some accounts say that Gustav, on occasion, refused to even acknowledge Arnold as his son.

The Nazi Question

The smudged outlines of Gustav Schwarzenegger's Nazi involvement emerged only years after his death, when Arnold Schwarzenegger asked an American organization dedicated to preserving the memory of the Holocaust to research his father's past. The research by the Simon Wiesenthal Center and documents that were sealed until thirty years after Gustav Schwarzenegger's death in 1972 show that the elder Schwarzenegger had joined the Nazi Party in 1938. The elder Schwarzenegger volunteered to be a member of the Sturmabteilung, or storm troopers, a notorious organization that played a critical role in expanding Hitler's power. He joined the brownshirts, as the storm troopers were called, in 1939, about six months after the troopers participated in one of the most infamous chapters of the war's innumerable atrocities. The brownshirts played a pivotal role in the bloody Kristallnacht riots, which destroyed more than one thousand synagogues, took tens of thousands of Jewish men to concentration camps, and led to the murders or suicides of hundreds of Jews. In 1942, after seeing military action in Poland, France, Lithuania, and Russia, the elder Schwarzenegger was wounded. A year and a half later, after suffering from repeated bouts of malaria, he was discharged. And in 1947 the Austrian authorities, having found no evidence that Gustav Schwarzenegger had committed war crimes, determined that he could work as a police officer in Thal.

The elder Schwarzenegger's Nazi past has trailed his son throughout his life. Questions about Arnold Schwarzenegger's beliefs about Hitler and Nazis, Jews and African Americans, surfaced during his California governor's campaign more than half a century later. "We cannot hold the son responsible for the misdeeds of his father," Rabbi Marvin Hier, the Wiesenthal Center's founder, has said. But Arnold Schwarzenegger himself has fueled some of the questions with remarks he has made about blacks, a Nazi salute he reportedly gave at a German contest, and a toast he offered at his wedding reception in honor of a high-ranking Austrian official who had been accused of Nazi atrocities. Years later Schwarzenegger apologized for the remark. In addressing the questions in a 2003 interview with the *Sacramento Bee* newspaper, Schwarzenegger said he was brought up surrounded by Austria's "unbelievable history of prejudice" but sought to become a different man after arriving in the United States. "I make myself go in the other direction than where I came from," he said.

Arnold's father Gustav was a Nazi storm trooper. Shown here is Gustav's military identification card.

The father regularly pitted the two boys against one another in contests of boxing, skiing, and other sporting events. "Let's see who's the best!"[7] Gustav Schwarzenegger would announce. Such competitions were only superficially sporting events; each boy believed he was battling to show his father he was the better son. The winner received lavish praise; the loser, humiliation. Arnold, the younger and more sickly of the two, won only occasionally.

The rigorous routines fashioned by Gustav Schwarzenegger turned even casual family outings into tests for his sons to prove themselves. He often required his sons to write detailed reports, ten pages long, on hikes or trips to museums and the like. Then, he meticulously graded the boys' reports, insisting that they write any misspelled words fifty times.

The zealous drive that became the essence of Arnold Schwarzenegger and revealed itself in all his life's pursuits was born in this family atmosphere. He was, as he once put it, hungrier for success than anyone he knew. "I didn't get certain things I needed as a child, and that, I think, finally made me hungry for achievement, for winning in other ways, for being the best, being recognized," he writes in his best-selling autobiography, *Arnold: The Education of a Bodybuilder.* "If I'd gotten everything and been well-balanced, I wouldn't have had my drive."[8]

Lofty Aspirations

Even as a young boy, Arnold Schwarzenegger harbored dreams as grandiose as Austria's imposing Alps, the mountains near his hometown. "When I was a small boy, my dream was not to be big physically, but big in a way that everybody listens to me when I talk, that I'm a very important person, that people recognize me and see me as something special," Schwarzenegger says. "I had a big need for being singled out."[9]

As teenagers, the Schwarzenegger boys, who by then attended the junior high school in Graz, the closest city, acquired reputations as local bullies. Once, the boys stole a classmate's books. Another time, they pummeled the milkman. Their police chief father, so strict at home, nonetheless protected his sons from village punishment for their pranks and violence.

Beginning early on, Arnold Schwarzenegger simply sought escape—from his father's strict discipline, from the stifling nature of village life, and from the provincial confines of even Austria itself. "Ever since I was a child, I would say to myself, 'There must be more to life than this,'"[10] he has said.

He found his outlet just a few miles away in the movie theaters of nearby Graz, Austria's largest city. There, he watched Johnny Weissmuller, the former American Olympic swimmer, play Tarzan. He watched bodybuilding champions American Steve Reeves and Great Britain's Reg Park play the role of Hercules. These men, who rode their muscles to fame, became his role models and, eventually, his inspiration to create a similar vehicle for his own burning ambitions: he would shape his muscles into a form that equaled or surpassed his on-screen heroes. From that moment when he began shaping his muscles, Arnold Schwarzenegger began shaping his destiny.

Schwarzenegger regularly escaped the drudgery of his home life at the local cinema. There, he began to idolize musclemen actors like the former Olympic swimmer Johnny Weissmuller.

An Introduction to Bodybuilding

Arnold and Meinhard, like most European children, played soccer. Even as a child Arnold did not find team sports gratifying. If his soccer team won, and he was not singled out for praise, he felt disappointed. But soccer introduced him to bodybuilding, the pursuit that captivated him like no other.

The boys' soccer coach began taking the team members to a gym for regular weight training to strengthen their legs. Schwarzenegger described that summer, when he turned fifteen and was introduced to the gym, as a magical season. It was then he discovered his life's ambition, to become the best-built man in the world.

"When I was fifteen, I had a dream that I wanted to be the best body builder in the world and the most muscular man," Schwarzenegger says. "It was not only a dream I dreamed at night. It was also a daydream. It was so much in my mind that I felt it had to become a reality."[11]

Hoisting Heavy Steel

Bodybuilding is a sport that dates back to the ancient Greeks. For bodybuilders, the goal of exercising is not health or fitness but looks: creating an ideal physique of sculpted muscles. Bodybuilding was far from a popular athletic pursuit when Arnold began devoting himself to it. The sport was widely ridiculed by people who considered bodybuilding competitions beauty pageants rather than true athletic endeavors. But Arnold, never one for following a crowd, was enchanted with everything about the obscure sport and the behemoth men who were its icons.

"I'm not exactly sure why I chose bodybuilding, except that I loved it," Arnold recalls. "I loved it from the first moment my fingers closed around a barbell and I felt the challenge and exhilaration of hoisting the heavy steel plates above my head."[12]

Decades later he still recalls, with excruciating detail, the experiences and aftermath of his first real workout in Graz, an eight-mile trip from his home. Arnold biked to the gym and then used barbells, dumbbells, and machines, leading experienced bodybuilders in the gym to warn the novice that he would be sore. Arnold dismissed their warnings. But he then discovered that he was too weak to bike home. His legs, he recalls, were reduced to noodles, and his hands were so flaccid they could no longer grip the handlebars.

> I was numb, my whole body buzzing. I pushed the bike for a while, leaning on it. Half a mile farther, I tried to ride it again, fell off again, and then just pushed it the rest of the way home. This was my first experience with weight training, and I was crazy for it. The next morning I couldn't even lift my arm to comb my hair. Each time I tried, pain shot through every muscle in my shoulder and arm. I couldn't hold the comb. I tried to drink coffee and spilled it all over the table. I was helpless.[13]

He also was transfixed by the men he saw in the gym. "Those guys were huge and brutal. . . . The weight lifters shone with sweat; they were powerful looking, Herculean," he recalls. "And there it was before me—my life, the answer I'd been seeking. It clicked. It was something I suddenly just seemed to reach out and find, as if I'd been crossing a suspended bridge and finally stepped off onto solid ground."[14]

Austrian Oak Story

With his bodybuilding success, Arnold Schwarzenegger acquired the nickname "the Austrian Oak." The name evoked both the image of his sturdy, massive physique and the days of his youth, when he performed chin-ups from the limb of a tree that stood on the banks of the Thalersee, the lake of his hometown in Austria. In his 1993 book, *Arnold's Fitness for Kids Ages 11–14*, Schwarzenegger tells the story of his efforts to break the record of twenty-one chin-ups on the branch of one particular tree. The record was held by Franz Steeger, a local athlete. When the fourteen-year-old Schwarzenegger found he could not get beyond eighteen chin-ups, Steeger told him, "You do the rest with your mind," and launched into a pep talk about how Arnold would accomplish great things for himself and for the others in his village. It was an inspirational message that the bodybuilder never forgot.

In his book Schwarzenegger recalls what then took place:

> We walked together over to the chin-up tree and without saying anything to anyone, I dried my hands on my pants and jumped up and grabbed the limb. It felt like shaking hands with an old friend. I did the chin-ups slowly, clearing my chin well over the branch on each one and keeping my breathing regular and deep as I had learned to do. By the time I reached twelve or thirteen, it looked like everyone at the party had gathered around the tree and was listening to Franz count off the chin-ups. I got to seventeen without tiring. Eighteen was hard, but I did the nineteenth, the one I had been chasing for weeks. Then I thought I was finished, and I just hung from the branch looking up at it, wishing but not really believing that I could do three more. "Now you do it with your mind, Arnold," said Franz quietly. I have thought of that many times since. Whenever I have been faced with something I thought I couldn't do in life, I have heard Franz Steeger's calm voice say, "Now you do it with your mind, Arnold."

Schwarzenegger broke the record that day, completing twenty-two chin-ups from the branch of the Austrian tree.

A Pursuit Becomes a Passion

Though his schoolmates and parents dismissed his budding passion as crazy, Arnold soon began making the trip to the gym, usually on foot or by bicycle, six days a week. His parents, worried that his enthusiasm was becoming an obsession, limited him to three visits per week. But when faced with the curfew, Arnold turned a room of the house into a gym. Though the room was unheated, leading Arnold to train in icy cold conditions during the Bavarian winters, he later called the location perfect because of the thick, centuries-old walls and sturdy floors that could withstand the punishment wrought by the weights.

Arnold saw most of his idols only on the movie screen or in the pages of muscle magazines, but one famed Austrian bodybuilder lived practically next door, in Graz. Kurt Marnul, "Mr.

Bodybuilding became an obsession for Schwarzenegger as he strove for excellence in the sport. He is pictured here in 1978, during a workout.

Austria," ran the Athletic Union Graz, a gym where that nation's best bodybuilders trained. Upon learning that the swim master at Thal's picturesque lake, the Thalersee, was a friend of Marnul's, Arnold pleaded for an introduction. Finally, Marnul agreed, meeting his devoted fan when he went to the Thalersee for a swim. Though Marnul initially thought Meinhard's broad shoulders and narrow hips made him a more promising bodybuilder, he invited both Schwarzeneggers to train in his gym. Soon it was clear that Arnold was the more ambitious. The very next morning Marnul found Arnold waiting for him on the gym's doorstep.

In that primitive gym Arnold first received the training advice that would take him to the pinnacles of the sport. "When you train, think of the muscle you are working on or developing and go to the farthest pain barrier," Marnul told him. "Go on until you cry out. That is the secret of the biggest bodybuilders. They train beyond the pain barrier."[15] Schwarzenegger embraced that philosophy throughout his bodybuilding career. He believed that a willingness to go beyond the pain barrier was the characteristic that distinguished a champion from all the rest. "That what most people lack is having the guts to go in and say I go through [the pain barrier] and I don't care what happens," he said in 1975, the year he won his sixth Mr. Olympia crown. "I have no fear of fainting in a gym because I know it could happen. I threw up many times when I was working out but it doesn't matter because it's all worth it."[16]

"I Knew I Was a Winner"

When Arnold began this intense pursuit, he was six feet tall and slender, weighing about 150 pounds. He fully intended to mold his physique into one that emulated or surpassed the rippling body of his idol, Reg Park. Arnold aimed to increase his weight to a massive 250 pounds. Within six years he achieved the goal, standing six feet two inches tall and weighing 250 pounds.

But as outsized—or outlandish—as his muscles became, they paled in comparison to the size of the ego and ambition that is quintessentially Arnold Schwarzenegger.

"I knew I was a winner," he writes in his autobiography. "I knew I was destined for great things. People will say that kind of thinking is totally immodest. I agree. Modesty is not a word that applies to me in any way—I hope it never will."[17]

His parents disapproved of his passion for bodybuilding. They considered it an obsession that was not normal, and Arnold later conceded that his parents had been right.

> Normal people can be happy with a regular life. I was different. I felt there was more to life than just plodding through an average existence. I'd always been impressed by stories of greatness and power. Caesar, Charlemagne, Napoleon were names I knew and remembered. I wanted to do something special, to be recognized as the best. I saw bodybuilding as the vehicle that would take me to the top, and I put all my energy into it.[18]

Total Dedication

Arnold's single-minded dedication to training has since acquired a mystique. Karl Kainrath, a bodybuilder who trained with Arnold at the Union, describes Arnold's determination by saying, "We all knew that the building could have fallen down, but Arnold would still have continued training."[19]

Schwarzenegger was so devoted to training that once he smashed a gym window to break into the facility so he could train on weekends when the facility was closed. He would choose to do the final set of weights even when it meant walking home after the final bus for home had departed. Once, in a story that would become part of the standard Schwarzenegger legend, he trained in such bitter cold that when he released the bar, he found his skin had ripped away, stuck to the frozen metal bar.

"His dedication was total, unswerving, and heroic," writes biographer Wendy Leigh. "He was almost a missionary in his attempt to convert his body into the perfect work of art he so passionately desired it to be. Nothing mattered anymore except training —not school, not friends, not girls, not his parents, nothing."[20]

Mental Prowess

If his devotion became legendary, so did his passion for the mental games he wielded in competition and in the gym. One of the most often-told stories of Arnold's training involves the cruel practical joke he played on an aspiring bodybuilder, seeking the secrets to Arnold's budding success at bodybuilding. According to biographer Wendy Leigh, Swarzenegger told the boy,

> "If you want to build a body like mine, you have to grind up nutshells and add them to a spoonful of salt. Eat one spoonful of this mixture on the first day. On the second day, increase it to two. On the third, three. And so on, until the thirtieth day, when you should be eating thirty teaspoons a day. Then you will put on a lot of muscle.". . . [The young bodybuilder] rushed out and began Arnold's salt diet, in his besotted state not realizing that a large amount of salt is lethal to the system of anyone, human or superman, and that even a small amount of salt is anathema to the bodybuilder, making his body retain the liquid that all bodybuilders are intent on eliminating.[21]

The salt diet prank, which ended with the sick young man on the brink of hospitalization, was only one of the opening acts of the psychological games that one day would be as integral to his bodybuilding competitions as his biceps. It offered an early glimpse of the psyching-out methods the bodybuilder would wield to vanquish other contenders.

In fact, one secret to his early success was the powerful, controversial, and dangerous potion that had swept the bodybuilding universe and would eventually plague virtually all professional sports. Marnul said he introduced the teenage Schwarzenegger to steroids, the controversial and dangerous man-made drugs that build muscles by acting like the body's natural male hormone. During his bodybuilding career, Schwarzenegger admitted to using limited amounts of steroids, downplaying their dangers. But later, as more became known about the dangers, he changed his mind about the drugs and counseled athletes to avoid them.

Going AWOL to Win

In 1965, after graduating from secondary school, Arnold entered the Austrian army to complete his one year of military service the government required. The military's regimentation appealed to Arnold, for he had already discovered that one of bodybuilding's essential elements was physical and mental discipline.

Not long after he began his basic training in Vienna, he received an invitation to compete in the junior division of the Mr. Europe bodybuilding competition in Stuttgart, Germany. Strict rules prohibited recruits from leaving during their six-week-long basic training for anything but a death in the family or other extreme emergency. But the tale of how Arnold Schwarzenegger went AWOL (absent without leave) to enter his first bodybuild-

Schwarzenegger went AWOL from the Austrian army to compete in the junior division of Mr. Europe, his first bodybuilding competition. He is pictured here later in his bodybuilding career.

ing contest offers a classic example of how far the young body-builder was willing to go to win.

Schwarzenegger literally crawled over the wall of the base, fleeing with only the clothes he was wearing and the money to pay for a ticket on a third-class train that made frequent stops. Arriving a day later, he borrowed posing trunks and body oil. For his posing routine, the series of theatrical postures that are the essence of bodybuilding competition, he improvised, stringing together stances he had seen of his hero, Reg Park, in muscle magazines. It worked. At age eighteen the AWOL trainee tank driver was named Mr. Europe Junior. It was the first of nineteen bodybuilding titles he would win in the course of fifteen years.

He borrowed money to pay for the trip back to the base, where army officials promptly threw him in jail for a week. After that, deciding that the teenager's victory lent prestige to the army, officers reneged on his punishment, gave him two days' leave, and ordered him to spend his afternoons training in the gym rather than cleaning and oiling tanks. From then on Arnold Schwarzenegger's military service was essentially confined to lifting weights for six hours a day and eating more food than had ever been available at home. Eventually, he says, the drill instructors actually praised his antics when trying to motivate the troops. "'You have to fight for your fatherland,' they said. 'You have to have courage. Look at what Schwarzenegger did just to win this title.'" Schwarzenegger recalls the adulation saying, "I became a hero even though I had defied their rules to get what I wanted."[22]

When he returned home with his bodybuilding title his mother, at least, was a convert. She ran through Thal to show everyone her son's trophy. Shortly after his military service was completed, Schwarzenegger left Thal for good and headed for a job running a health club in Munich, Germany, his sights set on capturing bodybuilding's highest crowns.

"I was like a black trying to get out of Harlem," Schwarzenegger later recalled. "I knew when I left home that I'd never go back except as a visitor. On the train, leaving, I looked back and knew, it wasn't home anymore."[23]

Chapter 2

The Austrian Oak

AT AGE NINETEEN, with just a few titles under his belt, Arnold Schwarzenegger embarked on the first airplane flight of his life. With his fare scraped together by a collection from fellow bodybuilders at the Munich gym he managed, Schwarzenegger headed for London, his sights set on one of bodybuilding's highest crowns, Mr. Universe. "I hadn't been willing to work my way up through the countless little Mr. Thises and Mr. Thats," Schwarzenegger wrote in his autobiography more than a decade later. "I was shooting for the top."[24]

One of his early backers, a bodybuilding judge who had offered him the Munich job, had believed the young and inexperienced Schwarzenegger might be content to watch the competition. That assumption betrayed how little he understood of the competitor beneath the emerging layers of muscle. Never one for sitting on the sidelines, Schwarzenegger responded to the suggestion by asking, "What do you mean, *watch*?"[25]

At the time he entered the 1966 contest Schwarzenegger was struggling both to make ends meet and to find the time for the intensive weight training his pursuit required. He loathed the work at the health club, where he gave advice to clients who put themselves through routines he disdained as superficial, "sissy workouts."[26] But the job proved the catalyst for what would become the signature split training regimen he followed for years. Initially out of necessity, in order to accommodate his working hours, Schwarzenegger began training from nine to eleven in the morning and again from seven to nine in the evening. Despite the naysayers who predicted Schwarzenegger's overtraining would lead his muscles to deteriorate, he stuck to it long after circumstances demanded it. He would eventually look back on his effort, comparing his weight lifting to the work of artists. "I felt like Leonardo Da Vinci," he says. "I was a sculptor sculpting the body."[27]

Aiming for Mr. Universe

When he flew to London, he had not yet learned to capitalize on the withering mind games that one day would be as famed, and as critical to his success, as his twenty-two-inch biceps and

Peak Measurements

When he was at the peak of his form, Arnold Schwarzenegger stood six feet two inches tall, weighed 235 pounds, had biceps as big around as a small woman's waist, and thighs nearly as big around as a basketball. His body measurements, in circumference, were: biceps, 22 inches; calves, 20 inches; chest, 57 inches; waist, 34 inches; and thighs, 28 1/2 inches.

Schwarzenegger poses here at Muscle Beach in Santa Monica, California. His huge, sculpted body inspired awe.

twenty-inch calves. Combing over pictures of previous years' top finalists, Schwarzenegger conceded to himself that he simply could not beat them. It was one of the few times in his life that Schwarzenegger allowed himself to confront defeat as a likely outcome. "It was a loser's way of looking at it," he later said. "I defeated myself before I even entered. . . . I hadn't yet pulled together my ideas about the powers of the mind over the muscles."[28]

He arrived in London, his only English a memorized sentence to ask the taxi driver to take him to the Royal Hotel. Though he first wound up at the wrong hotel and then came in second in the contest, Schwarzenegger nonetheless captured the Mr. Universe title "in all but name,"[29] as one biographer puts it. He won two curtain calls, a standing ovation, and his first measure of fame. He had served notice that he was clearly Europe's rising bodybuilding star. People began to call him "the Austrian Oak," a reference to his towering physique, and a nod to the Thalersee trees whose limbs had served as Schwarzenegger's early chin-up bars.

"Of course, he was young and had all the right measurements. But that wasn't it," Jimmy Savile, a British disc jockey who headed a bodybuilder's organization, says of Schwarzenegger's London debut. "It was his incredible personality. When he came onstage, it was like somebody had turned on all the spotlights. He just lit the stage up."[30]

The next year Schwarzenegger won the crown, becoming at age twenty the youngest Mr. Universe in history.

Growing Success

At the time of his growing European success, Schwarzenegger says he felt superior to everyone, as if he were indeed a superman. He acquired a collection of speeding tickets, a record for getting into scrapes with policemen, and a reputation for being easily provoked into fights. He was, he says, trying to prove through rudeness how much of a man he was. Years later, he explained his reckless behavior by using an analogy with cars:

> When you have a BMW, which drives well although it's
> not a great car, you try to race with everybody to prove

Exuberant after winning the 1967 Mr. Universe title, Schwarzenegger pretends to drink a toast from his trophy while wearing its cap as a crown.

that it has speed. But when you have a Ferrari or a Lamborghini you *know* you can beat anybody on the street. . . . You *know* how good you are, you don't have to prove it anymore. It was the same for that period in my life. I wanted to think I was the greatest bodybuilder but I wasn't. Not yet. Not even in my mind. That's why I had to spend every minute trying to prove it.[31]

With characteristic rigor, Schwarzenegger began to focus on showmanship, an ingredient as essential as muscles in the theatrical spectacles that are bodybuilding competitions. He began posing to music, adopting the dramatic song from the movie

The "Pump" Defined

The 1977 movie, *Pumping Iron*, turned an obscure phrase into the lexicon of pop culture. The iron, of course, refers to the weights bodybuilders use, and pumping refers to lifting the weights. In George Butler's book, *Arnold Schwarzenegger: A Portrait*, Schwarzenegger offers his definition of the "pump":

"Not many people understand what a pump is. It must be experienced to be understood. It is the greatest feeling I get. I search for this pump because it means that my muscles will grow when I get it. I get a pump when the blood is running into my muscles. They become really tight with blood. Like the skin is going to explode any minute. It's like someone putting air in my muscles. It blows up. It feels fantastic."

Exodus as his theme. At demonstrations he dictated the lighting and the rise and fall of the curtain. He eventually studied ballet.

Authors Robert Lipsyte and Peter Levine observe in their book *Idols of the Game* that

> Bodybuilding contests maintain, as do figure skating and beauty pageants, a veneer of empirical criteria that masks the outcome's large subjective nature. One of Schwarzenegger's greatest skills was manipulating that outcome, which at times was as simple as having the backdrop color change to better contrast his skin tone and blur the definition of a darker-skinned rival.[32]

The years bodybuilders spend embracing the pain and monotony of weight lifting culminate in theatrical presentations onstage in competitions that extend for just minutes. Judges look for a body that is muscular, proportioned, and symmetrical. To best display themselves, bodybuilders shave away all body hair, oil their skin, and wear only small trunks. They want to show what in the jargon of the sport is called "definition." That is, they want their muscles to be as visible as possible. They want the muscles to be mapped with veins—not for beauty per se, but to show there is no layer of fat obscuring the blood vessels that lie between the skin and muscles. Schwarzenegger himself used a simple test to see how much fat was on his body: He only needed to jump up and down and watch what jiggled. He passed his own test. When he jumped, nothing jiggled.

Posing like a Big Cat

Bodybuilders in competitions display themselves in stances called poses. The poses take their names from the muscles they emphasize, such as the back double-biceps or the kneeling side chest. The pose is considered the heart of the bodybuilding pursuit.

Schwarzenegger strikes an impressive pose in a 1967 photo. In competition, bodybuilders stage posing presentations in order to display their physiques to the judges.

"Depending on how it is done, you can see in it either everything that is moving and beautiful and dignified about the display of a developed male body or everything that is ridiculous and embarrassing about it,"[33] explain Charles Gaines and George Butler, who collaborated on the 1974 book *Pumping Iron: The Art and Sport of Bodybuilding.*

Schwarzenegger strove to make his posing presentations something so unique they simply said, "Arnold." He wanted his presentations to be both powerful and graceful. To that end he took inspiration from movements of the big cats that jump gracefully and land with force to kill. Even in the early days of his career Schwarzenegger showed a flair for adapting his routine to the tastes of his audiences—artistic poses he felt best suited audiences in sophisticated Paris, and brutal presentations he felt better adapted to brash New York. A striking example of his improvisational cunning came in Schwarzenegger's first moments on stage in Brooklyn, New York, at the 1973 Mr. Olympia contest, the fourth of seven times he would win the crown. Charles Gaines writes of the event:

> In a madness of noise, an ear-splitting, wall-shaking tumult of noise, he takes the stage, his face radiant, and shows the audience and judges—a single leg. It is the leg he injured a few months earlier when a posing platform in South Africa collapsed with him, and he wants them to see that it is as good as ever. He turns it languidly, showing the elegant complexity of his calf. Then he cuts to a front double-biceps—a pose that shows the entire front of the body. From zoom to pan, from detail to mind-blowing whole . . . it impales the crowd.[34]

The Master Plan

In September 1968, after winning his second Mr. Universe title in Great Britain, twenty-one-year-old Arnold Schwarzenegger flew to America to prove himself again in the land he had so long dreamed of conquering. He intended to vanquish the U.S. bodybuilders just as he had those in Europe. He intended to become the unrivaled brand name in bodybuilding. "I wanted every single person who touched a weight to equate the feeling of the barbell with my name,"[35] as he puts it. And that was only the beginning.

Long before he ever set foot on American soil, Schwarzenegger had created for himself what he called, "the Master Plan." The plan was an incredibly detailed and stunningly ambitious blueprint for all Schwarzenegger aimed to achieve in life. He planned to become the greatest bodybuilder in history. He planned to learn English and to learn the basics of business. He planned to make a fortune by investing his bodybuilding earnings in real estate. After his bodybuilding career, he intended to take Hollywood by storm, first starring in movies and later directing and producing them. By age thirty he intended to be a millionaire and movie star. Because he considered money the most obvious source of power, he planned to acquire all the trappings of great wealth—houses, cars, art. He planned to marry a glamorous and intelligent woman, and by age thirty-two he planned to have been invited to the White House.

"What made this plan difficult was the nature of the fellow in charge of it," says George Butler, who made *Pumping Iron* and explains the Master Plan's details in a photography book of Schwarzenegger.

> Arnold was hard to imagine, much less deal with in the flesh. Most people were affronted by him; others laughed at him behind his back. As late as the mid-seventies it was impossible for anyone in the world to believe that a man who was once a poor, uneducated immigrant could use *his muscles* as the foundation for a plan to exemplify Making It in America. Given what he began with, it was the most difficult means to an end imaginable. But not for Arnold. His fate was as clear as his view of himself in the old gym mirror. He knew he could control what he saw there, and it was his plan to do the same with his life.[36]

Twenty Dollars and a Gym Bag

Schwarzenegger first arrived in the United States, the land of his dreams, in September 1968 with twenty dollars, his gym bag, a

Governor-elect Schwarzenegger poses with Joe Weider, the creator of the Olympia bodybuilding competition, who was instrumental in furthering Schwarzenegger's bodybuilding career.

tiny bit of English, and, as one biographer put it, "his home-grown arrogance."[37]

He had one other asset: the patronage of Joe Weider, America's impresario of bodybuilding. A shrewd businessman who had created an empire of publishing muscle magazines, selling bodybuilding products, and sponsoring bodybuilding contests, Weider brought Schwarzenegger to America with a contract. In exchange for promoting Weider's products and events, Schwarzenegger received a salary, an apartment, and a car. The contract itself signaled Weider's belief in Schwarzenegger's potential.

"There was absolutely no question that Arnold was a sleeping giant just waiting to be roused to reach the greatness he was slated for,"[38] Weider later said. Weider immediately sensed that Schwarzenegger's exceptional willpower, charm, and drive to win distinguished him from the pack. "I knew, and he knew, that he could be great," he said. "We created Arnold."[39]

Just one day after his arrival in America, a pale, jet-lagged Schwarzenegger, then twenty-one, lost the Mr. Olympia contest to American bodybuilder Frank Zane.

"He slinked back to his hotel room, humiliated and far from home, and cried himself to sleep," biographer Robert Lipsyte writes. "That was probably the worst it ever got for Arnold Schwarzenegger."[40]

The Golden State

Under Weider's patronage Schwarzenegger trained in the famed Gold's Gym in Santa Monica, California, which became a storied site for bodybuilders. The nearby beach became so identified with bodybuilders that people referred to it as Muscle Beach. In California Schwarzenegger found all the qualities that matched the vision of America he created for himself when he was a boy in Austria.

"California is to me a dreamland," he said. "It is the absolute combination of everything I was always looking for. It has all the money in the world there, show business there, wonderful weather there, beautiful country, ocean is there. . . . You have beautiful-looking people there. They all have a tan."[41]

Once there, Schwarzenegger began a self-improvement plan that extended well beyond his muscles. He lifted weights, but also took college courses at a community college, studying algebra, for instance, and basic English. Over the years, in fact, he would repeat the phrase "thirty-three thousand, three hundred thirty-three and one-third" to pronounce the "th" sound of English—a step aimed at eliminating his trademark Austrian accent, and perhaps one of the very few lifelong goals Schwarzenegger failed to fully achieve.

Frank Zane, who would go on to be a three-time Mr. Olympia, trained with Schwarzenegger in those early days. A former math teacher, he tutored Schwarzenegger in algebra for a Santa Monica City College course. After an hour of working on algebra problems, Zane suggested that they stop, but Schwarzenegger insisted on working for another half an hour. When the two would train with weights, they often used a technique they called

The Ideal Strongman

When Mr. Olympia is crowned each year, he receives a statuette of a Victorian man wearing only a mustache and a fig leaf. He is modestly muscled by modern standards. In one hand he grips an old-fashioned globe barbell. The other hand extends gracefully. The statuette is called the Sandow, and it is named for Eugen Sandow, considered one of the first modern bodybuilders.

Sandow was born in 1897 in Prussia, a region that is now part of Germany. He had both the physique and flair for showmanship that made bodybuilding a turn-of-the-century phenomenon. Sandow made his name in Europe by defeating another well-known strongman. Believed at the time to be the world's most perfectly developed man, he wowed Europe to such a degree that the king of England eventually made him his special instructor in physical culture. He became a hit in America, too. His stunts are legendary. In one publicity photo, Sandow is shown in a squat position, his hands on his upper thighs, as he lifts nineteen people and a dog, all of them standing on a beam laid across his shoulders. He was a shrewd businessman, too, opening a chain of fitness salons, inventing bodybuilding gizmos (Sandow's Patented Health Corset) and concoctions (Sandow's Health and Strength Cocoa).

On September 14, 1901, Sandow held an event he called "The Great Competition," the first major physique competition the world had ever seen. Men wearing black tights, leather belts, and leopard skin loin-

cloths competed before standing-room-only crowds in a London auditorium. The winners were awarded statuettes of an ideal strongman, Sandow himself. Replicas of those statuettes began to be used again in 1980 in the Mr. Olympia contests—an idea in part attributed to Arnold Schwarzenegger.

Eugen Sandow, one of the first modern bodybuilders, is pictured here in 1890.

"forced repetitions," using a spotter to help them keep lifting weights beyond the point when the muscles had reached their limit. "I'm going to do forced repetitions,'" Schwarzenegger told Zane, applying the bodybuilding phrase to the task of algebra. "He's like that with everything," Zane says. "He is fierce. Nobody is more focused than him."[42]

Mr. Olympia

In 1969, after a year of training, Schwarzenegger lost two more key competitions to Cuban bodybuilder Sergio Oliva. But the following year he finally won the coveted Mr. Olympia, a title he eventually would claim for a then-unprecedented seven times in all. From that day on, Schwarzenegger emerged the victor in all the bodybuilding contests he entered.

Schwarzenegger reached two bodybuilding milestones in 1970. In London, Schwarzenegger won the Mr. Universe contest, defeating his boyhood idol, Reg Park, who had staged a comeback more than twenty years after his bodybuilding debut. Then he defeated Oliva for the first time. The 1970 victory over Oliva was a study in the changed Schwarzenegger from their premier match the year before. In their 1969 competition Oliva had proved himself as one of the rare competitors who could psych out Schwarzenegger. Backstage, before the judging for the event began, Oliva had ever so casually flexed his muscles in Schwarzenegger's direction. The subtle display so deflated Schwarzenegger that he later admitted he felt defeated even before he stepped on the stage. But a year later, Schwarzenegger, who had reinvigorated his weight-lifting schedule to prepare, also began using the mental tools that would prove to be his muscles' essential competitive companion.

In their book *Idols of the Game* Robert Lipsyte and Peter Levine relate how the 1970 Mr. Olympia competition proved as much a mental contest as a physical one. Leading up to the final "pose down" between the two elaborately muscled men, Oliva furiously pumped weights in a burst of last-minute preparation. He was stunned, then, to see the nonchalance of Schwarzenegger, who casually strolled out for french fries, a calculated move intended to convey his cool. In the pose down that followed, Schwarzenegger

unleashed a strategic ploy that would become one of the most storied moments in his bodybuilding career. As the crowd shrieked
over the two behemoth men Schwarzenegger whispered to Oliva,
"I'm tired. Let's stop now." Oliva agreed. "You lead off," Schwarzenegger told him. With the crowd still begging for more, both
men began walking off the stage. But when Oliva reached the
wings Schwarzenegger returned to the stage, where he continued
to pose alone, earning more ecstatic applause—and in the end,
victory. "It was this kind of hunger for glory, loyalty to the crowd,
and showmanship over any sportsman's code that set Schwarzenegger apart and propelled him to the top."[43]

Pumping Iron

For years Arnold was the phenomenon of the bodybuilding
world, but his fame catapulted him beyond that subculture.
George Butler, a freelance photographer, and his writing partner, Charles Gaines, made Schwarzenegger the star of their 1974
book, *Pumping Iron.* Three years later, Butler turned the subject
into a documentary film of the same name. The film's popularity catapulted Schwarzenegger and the sport of bodybuilding itself into the broad public eye.

In the movie Schwarzenegger plays what reviewers later said
was the most fascinating role of his career: himself. The movie
follows the training of a select group of competitors in the 1975
Mr. Olympia contest in South Africa. Schwarzenegger won the
title as much with his mental techniques as his physical attributes. According to one reviewer, "Larger than life, though not
necessarily larger than his rivals for the Mr. Universe and Mr.
Olympia bodybuilding titles (especially a young Lou Ferrigno,
hot on Arnold's competitive trail but much less interesting),
Schwarzenegger still comes across, at age twenty-eight, as a con-
summate politician, smart, likable, and crafty about exploiting
others' psychological weaknesses."[44]

In the movie Schwarzenegger smiles slyly as he explains his
methods:

> You have to do everything possible to win no matter
> what. The day of the contest if [a competitor] comes in

Schwarzenegger displays a T-shirt bearing his likeness at the premiere of the 1977 documentary film Pumping Iron, *in which Arnold starred.*

his best shape and he's equally as good as I am or if he's a few percent better than I am, I spend with him one night. . . . I book us in a room together, you know, to help him for tomorrow's contest. And that night he will never forget. I will mix him up. He will come so ready to South Africa, so strong. By the time the night is over, the next morning he will be ready to lose. . . . I mean, I will just talk him into that. That's no problem to do.[45]

In the most controversial scene of the movie Schwarzenegger tells about missing his father's funeral in order to maintain his focus for an upcoming bodybuilding competition. Schwarzenegger and Butler later said the scene was an improvised bit of fiction, a moment Schwarzenegger created for its dramatic impact after the two had discussed another bodybuilder who had skipped his father's funeral. Nonetheless, Schwarzenegger did not attend the funeral of his father, who died of a stroke in 1972, or the funeral of his brother Meinhard, who died in a car accident in 1971.

Transcending Perceptions

The popularity of the movie transformed both the image of Schwarzenegger and the public perceptions of bodybuilding itself. Bodybuilding at the time was ridiculed. George Butler recalls,

> Back in the early 70's bodybuilding was the least glamorous sport in the world. The prevailing view was that it was purely homosexual, that bodybuilders were totally uncoordinated, and that when they grew older their muscles would turn to fat and that they had no intelligence whatsoever. Charles Gaines said that it was like trying to promote midget wrestling. It was so tawdry . . . everyone we knew was laughing at us.[46]

In the intervening years, the atmosphere changed dramatically. Health clubs became ubiquitous. The quest for physical fitness grew into a sort of national obsession. Diets, supplements, and surgeries that promised to reduce weight appeared in advertising everywhere.

"These days, 50 million people in America are lifting weights," Butler says. "When we started *Pumping Iron*, I could go to three gyms in New York, and two of them were half closed. Now there are 2,000 gyms in the New York metropolitan area."[47]

Schwarzenegger almost singlehandedly transformed the sport. According to Charles Gaines, "America discovered bodybuilding because it happened to lie next to Arnold Schwarzenegger."[48]

Robert Lipsyte and Peter Levine write,

> *Pumping Iron* plugged into a rebirth of physical culture in America that began in the sixties. The American peo-

ple's fascination with Schwarzenegger translated into fascination with themselves, which in turn fed their fascination back to him. People began to imagine possibilities for their own quads and lats, and they yearned to feel powerful. . . . On any given day you can turn on a cable television sports channel and see men and women bodybuilders in action, thanks to Schwarzenegger.[49]

Perfect Timing

Schwarzenegger seized the moment. He capitalized on the passion for improved fitness that the movie had inspired by publishing a book, a combination autobiography and training manual. The book became a best-seller, and he eventually followed up that success with a series of fitness manuals, each targeted at different audiences.

Catapulted to prominence by the movie, Schwarzenegger rapidly grew from cult figure into pop culture icon, the subject of rich impersonations by comics. Perhaps the most memorable Schwarzenegger caricature became a long-running gag on the hip comedy show, *Saturday Night Live.* Clad in preposterously overstuffed gray sweatsuits, comedians Dana Carvey and Kevin Nealon played "Hans and Franz," bodybuilders with thick Bavarian accents who disparaged less powerful males as "girly men," and introduced themselves by saying, "We're here to pump you up!" punctuated with a clap between the words "pump" and "you."

Visualizing Power

Even before his widespread fame, Schwarzenegger was sure of where he would go in life. When the *Pumping Iron* team first met Schwarzenegger, he told them of the importance of looking in the mirror and visualizing what one could be. The filmmakers immediately understood that his vision of himself extended far beyond the gym.

"He told us of a recurring dream," George Butler writes. "In it, he was king of all the earth and everyone looked up to him."[50]

In the movie itself, Schwarzenegger reveals that the power that transfixed him went well beyond physical definitions. "I was always dreaming about very powerful people, dictators and things like that," he says. "I was just always impressed by people who would be remembered for hundreds of years or even like Jesus, you know, being remembered for thousands of years."[51]

In order to raise the money to make *Pumping Iron*, Butler had courted myriad financial backers. After the film was released he took Schwarzenegger to a lunch with one of them, a wealthy

Steroids

Steroids are man-made chemicals that mimic the hormone testosterone and build muscle. They are powerful, dangerous, and sometimes illegal drugs. Though steroid use is banned from virtually all sporting endeavors, the drugs continue to be a controversial presence in amateur and professional athletics.

During his bodybuilding career Arnold Schwarzenegger admitted to using steroids in limited amounts. "I take steroids because they help me an extra 5 percent," he told television journalist Barbara Walters in a 1974 interview. An account of that interview appears in George Butler's book, *Arnold Schwarzenegger: A Portrait*. Schwarzenegger said, "I do it under a doctor's supervision. These steroids are mild and I do not know an intelligent builder who has been hurt by them."

Schwarzenegger's admission was unusual. At that time, though the drugs were ubiquitous in the sport, most bodybuilders publicly denied using them. Also, few understood the drugs' potential long-term health dangers.

Since then, scores of studies have documented a long list of the health hazards associated with steroid use. The drugs can stunt growth, lead to cancer, ruin the liver, cause heart disease and stroke, and lead to violent outbursts.

Steroid use remains a scourge of sports. In the 1990s steroid use among high school and middle school students soared to such a degree that in 2000 the National Institute on Drug Abuse launched a campaign to combat the trend. In 2003 major league baseball found that one in twenty of its players had used muscle-building drugs, leading many to question whether recent record-breaking baseball achievements were the result of steroids. The same year, an international investigation of drug use in athletics began when U.S. officials learned of an entirely new and illegal steroid that had been designed specifically to evade detection in standard medical tests.

Schwarzenegger has changed his opinion about the use of steroids from the one he expressed during his bodybuilding heyday. "Because of the health risk that's been proven they present, I strongly feel there is no place for them in bodybuilding or any sport, especially among competitive professionals," he wrote to a fan on his website in 2000.

Wall Street investor who invited business colleagues to join them. To Butler's amusement, Schwarzenegger began lecturing the group, an assemblage of some of the nation's most successful financial investors—not on bodybuilding, but on business. Decades later Butler recalled the meeting, saying with a chuckle, "Arnold has outperformed each one of those guys. I know he's wealthier than anyone at the table that day."[52]

As Far as He Can Go

But there were many people who did not think Schwarzenegger was capable of achieving more than the fame *Pumping Iron* brought him. In 1976, to promote *Pumping Iron*, Schwarzenegger and two other bodybuilders posed in a strange exhibition at New York City's Whitney Museum of American Art. The largest crowd to attend any event in the museum's history turned out to see the three bodybuilders pose, along with slides projecting images of sculptures by Rodin and Michelangelo.

After the show Butler shared a taxi with Candace Bergen, an actress who had attended the show. She told him, "You know, George, Arnold and bodybuilding have peaked. It's all gone about as far as it can." Butler disagreed, saying, "It's here to stay and Arnold is going to be the governor of California one day."[53]

Chapter 3

Going Hollywood

Arnold Schwarzenegger's 1970 movie debut did not portend the arrival of an actor destined to become an international star. His first movie went by several names, sometimes *Hercules in New York*, sometimes *Hercules—the Movie*, or sometimes, *Hercules Goes Bananas*. In search of a muscled actor who could play Hercules, the hero of Greek mythology, the movie's producers sought recommendations from Joe Weider, the businessman at the helm of a bodybuilding empire and Schwarzenegger's sponsor. Weider suggested they give the role to Schwarzenegger. "(The producers) asked me if he could act," Weider recalls. "I said 'Of course he can, in England he was a Shakespearean actor.' And they fell for it."[54]

Schwarzenegger was not allowed to use his real last name because its four syllables were thought to be too long and too cumbersome. He was not allowed to use his own voice, either, because of his thick Austrian accent. So, he went by the stage name of Arnold Strong, and another actor dubbed Schwarzenegger's lines. Still, Schwarzenegger was thrilled with the opportunity:

> Imagine coming to this country in late 1968 and then getting a phone call a few months later saying we want you to star in a Hercules movie. . . . I couldn't believe it, because this is only the kind of things you read about and you say this thing is fake. I was a farm boy coming off the boat from Austria, and here I was asked to star in a film. I thought this was a great beginning, even though I didn't know what I was doing.[55]

The low-budget, seventy-five-minute-long movie allowed Schwarzenegger to fulfill a lifelong fantasy, to play the same character he had watched his boyhood idols Steve Reeves and Reg Parks portray on the movie theater screens in Graz. In the 1970 version featuring Schwarzenegger, Hercules is expelled from Mount Olympus and lands in 1960s New York City penniless and wearing only a toga. A description of the movie from the film's distributor declares: "The action never stops. [Hercules] is chased by beautiful girls, fight promoters, grizzly bears,

Schwarzenegger began his movie career in 1978 by starring in the low-budget action movie Hercules in New York.

gangsters and an angry Zeus hurling thunderbolts, all culminating in an uproarious chariot race through Times Square."[56] The movie would be completely forgotten were it not for its role as the motion picture vehicle that launched Schwarzenegger's acting career. Occasionally the movie surfaces on late-night television, occasions that have been reported to prompt scores of Schwarzenegger's friends to call, laughing over his film debut.

Trying Again

Three years later, Schwarzenegger appeared in his second film with a small forgettable role in *The Long Goodbye*. Robert Altman, who had already won an Academy Award nomination for the critically acclaimed movie *M*A*S*H* three years earlier, directed the film, and actor Elliot Gould, a star who recently had been featured on the cover of *Time* magazine as an icon of the era, played the leading man. Schwarzenegger played a bit part as a deaf and mute hit man for the mob. "I didn't have to worry about forgetting my lines," he wisecracks. "I didn't have any!"[57] Decades later, long after Schwarzenegger's fame was established and Altman himself had won more critical acclaim, the director recalled the muscled actor he had hired sight unseen, saying, "I never would have forecast his success."[58]

Though the movie industry viewed Schwarzenegger as an outsider seeking to establish himself in an entirely new forum, in certain respects acting did not prove so far removed from bodybuilding, a sport in which the competitions themselves are performances and winning is heavily dependent on showmanship. "I was always fascinated with entertainment, with acting, with performing," Schwarzenegger says. "I think in my blood there's something that makes me want to be a performer. That's the way I was in bodybuilding. . . . The next natural step for me was to go into acting."[59]

In characteristic fashion, Schwarzenegger worked hard at making the transition. Over the years he took acting lessons, and he continued to work to eliminate his accent. Still, he found breaking into Hollywood a struggle against prevailing perceptions. "I experienced a *lot* of prejudice," he says. "The people in Hollywood had many reasons why I could not make it: my accent, my body, my long name. That made it very difficult—until I realized that you cannot compete at that level out here. You have to create your own position where you establish yourself in such a way that no one else can compete with you."[60]

The characteristics that initially were Schwarzenegger's liabilities grew into his trademarks, the very qualities that distinguished him from the pack. But as he sought to break into the business, he had to resist pressure to conform:

> I always felt the only way you make an impact is by doing things that have never been done before. "OK," I said. "If everyone has always changed their name, maybe I should be the first who doesn't change his name. If everyone has a perfect American accent to get to the top, maybe I should be the first who doesn't." I wanted to make sure that if I go on an elevator, before people ever saw me coming around the corner, they would say already, "That sounds like Arnold." I felt that my uniqueness would work to my advantage.[61]

In 1976, the year before he played himself in *Pumping Iron*, Schwarzenegger was cast as another bodybuilder, a fictional character in *Stay Hungry*. The movie featured two well-known

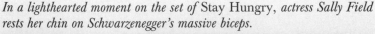

In a lighthearted moment on the set of Stay Hungry, *actress Sally Field rests her chin on Schwarzenegger's massive biceps.*

actors: Jeff Bridges, who had already been nominated for an Oscar for his role in *The Last Picture Show*, and Sally Field, then famed for playing the title roles in two popular television series, *Gidget* and *The Flying Nun*. In the movie Schwarzenegger plays Joe Santo, a bodybuilder who likes to work out in a rubber Batman suit. Though the film was a critical and commercial failure, it gave Schwarzenegger's budding acting career a boost because his performance won him the Golden Globe Award for Best New Male Star of the Year. Schwarzenegger even adopted the movie's title as a succinct life philosophy. Throughout his life he would say how important he found it to always set new challenges for himself, to "stay hungry."

Conan

In 1982 Schwarzenegger appeared in *Conan the Barbarian*, playing the title role of the pulp fiction hero featured in a series of books by Robert E. Howard. The movie, set in the mythical Hyborean Age twelve thousand years ago, follows Conan, a powerful man seeking revenge for the cruel deaths of his parents. The movie opens with the line, "That which does not kill you will make you strong," words written by German philosopher Friedrich Nietzsche, and, many observers have noted, a belief that parallels Schwarzenegger's own pain-embracing life philosophy.

> Conan was a man with a will and a character of steel and the whole movie had to do with steel . . . and with the sword . . . and the way you make a sword, in the most powerful and lasting way, is by heating it and pounding it, heating it, pounding it . . . so the more resistance it gets, the more pounding it gets, the stronger it gets, and this is also a representation of Conan. I understand this because of my early bodybuilding training. A person's character is like a muscle, the more resistance you give it, the better it grows, the stronger it grows.[62]

But the coveted role almost went to someone else because of a remark Schwarzenegger made that offended the movie's producer, Dino De Laurentiis. Meeting in the producer's office to discuss another possible movie, Schwarzenegger was surprised to

In 1982 Schwarzenegger starred in Conan the Barbarian. *Although the movie was a box-office hit, critics condemned Arnold's wooden performance and the film's gory action scenes.*

find a diminutive De Laurentiis working behind an enormous desk. "I said the first thing that came into my mind: 'God, why does a little man like you need such a huge desk?'" Schwarzenegger recalls. "And everybody in the office froze. He then tried to explain that he needs a big desk because he has so much work. . . . The meeting lasted one minute and forty seconds and afterward, my agent said, 'That was the worst thing I ever heard anybody say when he's trying to get a job.'"[63] John Milius, the movie's director, later persuaded De Laurentiis to cast Schwarzenegger despite the gaffe, arguing that the Austrian Oak, in effect, *was* Conan.

The filming, in Spain in 1981, was grueling. "On the first day I had to be attacked by wolves and fall from a high rock," Schwarzenegger recalls. "I landed on my back and had to have stitches. On the second day I had to fall into a cave. This time I hit my head and began bleeding. The director was delighted."[64]

The blood-soaked movie, a hit of the summer of 1982, established the "swords and sorcery" genre of films. Nevertheless, it was a critical failure, with reviewers castigating both its gore and Schwarzenegger's performance. *Time* magazine called *Conan* "a sort of psychopathic Star Wars, stupid and stupefying."[65] *Newsweek* described Schwarzenegger as "a dull clod with a sharp sword, a human collage of pectorals and latissimi who's got less style and wit than Lassie,"[66] a reference to the heroic collie of movie and television show fame. Even Schwarzenegger's mother, Aurelia, apparently disapproved, saying, "I hope it doesn't show in our village, the priest will be shocked."[67]

The Terminator

Undeterred by the extraordinarily withering reviews of his Conan character, in 1984 Schwarzenegger reprised his role. The sequel, *Conan the Destroyer*, proved even less popular and, impossible as it seems, even more critically disdained than the original. But the Conan sequel was eclipsed by another Schwarzenegger movie released the same year. It was *The Terminator*, the motion picture that sealed Schwarzenegger's fame and proved the turning point in his Hollywood career. He established himself as a star with a role in which he uttered a mere seventeen sentences. One of them, delivered in an emotionless monotone, became the signature line of his career: "I'll be back." The sentence, like the star himself, transcended moviemaking to become a part of the nation's pop culture lexicon.

The futuristic science-fiction thriller features Schwarzenegger in the title role. His Terminator is a cyborg, a killing machine,

The three wildly successful Terminator *films brought Schwarzenegger celebrity status and incredible wealth. He appears here in 2003's* Terminator 3.

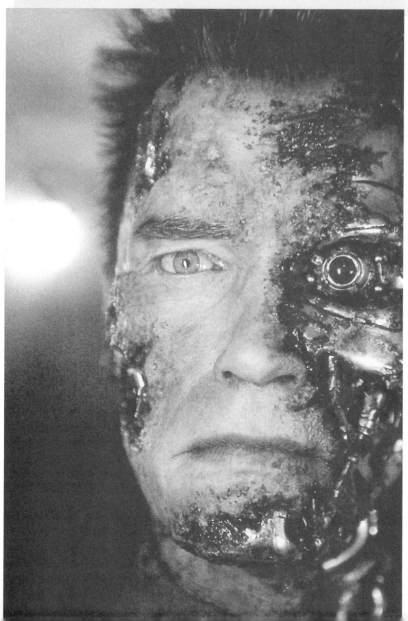

devoid of pain or emotion, that looks human. Schwarzenegger's cyborg and his adversary, a human hero, travel backward in time from a future nuclear-war-torn world in which machines have taken over and are trying to destroy what remains of humankind. The Terminator's mission is to alter history by killing the woman who will give birth to John Connor, the man destined to become leader of the human movement against the machines.

Originally, director James Cameron had intended to cast Schwarzenegger as the movie's hero, and former football-star-turned-actor O.J. Simpson as the villain. But after Schwarzenegger and Cameron met, the director is said to have exclaimed, "You are the Terminator!"[68] and both men left convinced that Schwarzenegger was best suited to play the evil Terminator instead.

Time magazine named it one of the best movies of 1984, and the *New York Times*'s Janet Maslin called it "A B-movie with flair."[69] The success of the movie and Schwarzenegger's memorable performance set the stage for the box office success that followed. Schwarzenegger's name, once considered too cumbersome for the general public, became a household word. His accent, once considered a liability, inspired countless celebrity imitators. Even his wooden acting style became, for at least this role, an asset.

Another Terminator

Though Schwarzenegger went on to star in more than a dozen other violent action movies and to take on a handful of comedy

Considering a Distant Future

Long before his movie career had been established in the roles of Conan or the Terminator, Arnold Schwarzenegger had begun thinking about an improbable subject: what he would do after stardom. Laurence Leamer's 1994 book, *The Kennedy Women*, reveals that in 1977, the year the film *Pumping Iron* was released, Schwarzenegger looked ahead in an interview with a German magazine, *Stern*. In prophetic remarks Schwarzenegger told the magazine, "When one has money, one day it becomes less interesting. And when one is also the best in film, what can be more interesting? Perhaps power. Then one moves into politics and becomes governor or president or something."

roles, the character of the cyborg Terminator proved his most successful and enduring creation. In 1991, seven years after the first *Terminator* movie, he returned to the role in the sequel, *Terminator 2: Judgment Day*. This time, his cyborg is a heroic machine on a mission to save thirteen-year-old John Connor from an even more advanced model of cyborg, T-1000, sent back from the future to kill the boy. The movie earned praise for its special effects and won four of the six Academy Awards for which it was nominated (one for makeup, one for visual effects, and two for sound and sound effects). The movie also gave Schwarzenegger another of his signature lines of dialogue: "Hasta la vista, baby." The line proved as enduring as *Casablanca*'s "Here's looking at you, kid."

In every respect, *Terminator 2* represents the pinnacle of Schwarzenegger's moviemaking career. It grossed $205 million in the United States alone, more than any other movie of that year, and more than any other movie in Schwarzenegger's decades-long career. Indeed, his pay for the movie suggests the heights he had scaled. For the role, Schwarzenegger received a $12 million jet and a percentage of the movie's total gross earnings. The movie, and Schwarzenegger himself, won over many critics. "Mr. Schwarzenegger's Terminator develops a gruff and winning kindliness that brings to mind John Wayne,"[70] Janet Maslin, the *New York Times* movie critic, observes. In his upbeat review (3½ of 4 possible stars), Roger Ebert, the Pulitzer Prize–winning movie critic of the *Chicago Sun-Times*, suggests the secret of Schwarzenegger's box office success: "Schwarzenegger's genius as a movie star is to find roles that build on, rather than undermine, his physical and vocal characteristics."[71]

The Height of Stardom

Four years after the first *Terminator* movie Schwarzenegger stood at the peak of his Hollywood career. In a four-year period he starred in five movies, all but one of them among the top ten moneymaking films for the years in which they were released. His salaries for movies soared along with his popularity, from the reported $250,000 he received for the first *Conan* movie to the reported $30 million he received for the third *Terminator* film. Schwarzenegger had become an extraordinarily wealthy man. In 1989 *Forbes* magazine listed him as one of the ten wealthiest entertainers in America, estimating that his income for the year would be $35 million. By 2003 the *Los Angeles Times* estimated that his fortune—built on the money he made in movies and real estate investments—exceeded $200 million.

As his success grew, he earned a reputation for being exceptionally controlling. "The only thing that makes me nervous is

Schwarzenegger greets his friend Danny DeVito at the premiere of Terminator 3. *The two actors starred as an unlikely pair of fraternal twins in the 1988 movie* Twins.

when I don't get my own way," he only half jokingly told an interviewer for *Playboy* magazine in 1988. The interview itself offered an example of just what he meant. He began the long question-and-answer session smoking a long, black Cuban Davidoff cigar, which he said had cost $25, and told reporter Joan Goodman, "Your time will be measured in stogies. When I finish one, the interview ends."[72]

Schwarzenegger's trademark role became the heroic character, and his trademark genre was the violent, action-packed movie. But in 1988 he made a switch, attempting his first comedy, *Twins.* The central gag of the movie is its casting, with the towering Schwarzenegger and the diminutive comic actor Danny DeVito cast as twins, born of a eugenics experiment and separated at birth. In 1990 he starred in *Kindergarten Cop*, appearing as a police detective who goes undercover as a kindergarten teacher. Though the movie itself is serious, it offers Schwarzenegger a number of comedic scenes with a room full of kindergarten students. Both movies were well received. "It was interesting to observe, while seeing the movie in a large audience, what genuine affection the public has for Schwarzenegger," critic Roger Ebert wrote. "He has a way of turning situations to his advantage, and creates an entertaining relationship with his young students in this movie."[73]

Schwarzenegger has said he tries to select roles he thinks the public will find in keeping with his established on-screen personas.

> I feel very much influenced by the public. . . . I know they like to see me do heroic movies and play a bigger-than-life, tough character. But at the same time they like to see me in funny circumstances. That's why the comedies *Twins* and *Kindergarten Cop*, work. I would not go in a direction that didn't work. Playing a junkie, lying in the gutter and shooting up with something, would not work. That I know for sure.[74]

Failure and Criticism

Yet for every Schwarzenegger movie blockbuster, there are more examples of failures. Many of his violent action movies and subsequent comedies proved box office disappointments and were disparaged by critics. He has on occasion joked about his failures. For instance, he acknowledges that his 1985 movie, *Red Sonja*, was the worst film he ever made. He says, "Now, when my kids get out of line, they're sent to their room and forced to watch Red Sonja ten times."[75]

Schwarzenegger as much as anyone appears to recognize his limitations in the craft of acting. "Many people still laugh at Schwarzenegger's often-wooden mannerisms and the absurd plots and over-the-top mayhem in his action movies," a book about the actor's films notes, "but as *The New York Times* observed in its review of *Kindergarten Cop* in 1990, 'no one laughs at Arnold Schwarzenegger better than Arnold Schwarzenegger himself.'"[76]

Though he has won worldwide celebrity and is frequently listed as one of the nation's favorite movie personalities, Schwarzenegger has never won the top acting awards. To the contrary, his idiosyncratic movies and demeanor have frequently made him the butt of jokes. For instance, while he has never been nominated for an Academy Award, he has been nominated seven times for a Razzie Award, given annually for the worst achievements in film. As of 2003, he held the record for most Razzie nominations without ever having won.

The same action movies that have won him fame have also brought him a degree of infamy. For instance, the National Coalition on Television Violence once gave Schwarzenegger a dubious distinction, naming him the most violent actor of the year based on his performance in the 1987 movie, *Running Man*, in which the character he plays averages 146 acts of violence per hour. An Internet site that chronicles violence in the movies once tallied up all of Schwarzenegger's "kills" from thirteen of the actor's movies over an eight-year period, beginning with the first Conan movie and ending with *Kindergarten Cop*. The total reached 446.

In a 1988 interview Schwarzenegger joked about the prevalence of violence in his movies, saying, "I have a love interest in every one of my films—a gun." And he dismissed the criticism. When asked whether his character sent the message that violence is heroic, Schwarzenegger replied, "No, because the bad

Rules for Playing the Hero

In a 1990 interview that appears in Nigel Andrews' book *True Myths: The Life and Times of Arnold Schwarzenegger*, Arnold Schwarzenegger explains the tiny details that are essential for portraying action heroes in the movies:

> There are a hundred rules for playing a hero. Never blink your eyes when you shoot—you look weak if the noise makes you blink. If you want to show power and anger convincingly, never move your head when you say your lines. John Wayne never moved his head. You can only move your lips; that shows you are ballsy. Show no emotions: You're above emotions. Never skip or hop; you must sprint or take powerful strides. When you are going up or down the stairs, never look at the stairs. . . . Every gesture has to separate you from the rest of the bunch if you want to play a stud.

Schwarzenegger attributes his success in action roles to his ability to act with an emotionless demeanor.

guys do worse. My characters just defend themselves. The message that is sent is to be strong and to be smart and to rely on yourself to get out of danger, to save your own life."[77]

Change of Heart

The birth of his four children, the first of them born in 1989, seemingly caused him to reconsider his earlier views and led him to try comedies.

> I start thinking about what kind of films they should see when they grew up. Do I want them to seek the ultimate violence in *Last Action Hero*? No, of course not. . . . I think

about the kids a lot. When [toy maker] Mattel came to me with the doll for Jack Slater [the character Schwarzenegger played in the 1993 box office failure, *Last Action Hero*], the first thing I said was I don't want to see a toy with a gun in its hand. Why not things to swing or climb with . . . ? Instead of a flame thrower, a fire extinguisher. Rather than destroy, have him protect. Make obstacles his challenge. So I think there is a lot of things I do now where being a father has made a difference.[78]

When the action-figure doll was released, the box was stamped with the slogan: "Play it smart. . . . Never play with real guns."[79]

Nonetheless, bloody action movies continued to be his Hollywood calling card. And in the fall of 2001, a strange blending of real-world violence and the fictional one Schwarzenegger's characters usually inhabit took place. On September 11 of that year, terrorists unleashed a horrific attack on the United States by steering commercial airplanes into New York City's World Trade Center and the Pentagon, the federal command station for the nation's military in Arlington, Virginia. At that time Warner Bros. was poised to release the movie *Collateral Damage*, starring Schwarzenegger as a firefighter who seeks revenge after his wife and child are killed in a terrorist bombing. The release was delayed until early the following year.

Stephen Hunter, a movie critic for the *Washington Post*, said the movie and Schwarzenegger seemed stale. "What is to become of Arnold Schwarzenegger?" Hunter asked. "It's a question this movie cannot help but raise."[80] Eighteen months later, Schwarzenegger would provide the answer to that very question.

Chapter 4

Marrying into American Royalty

A FRIEND ONCE asked a twenty-something Arnold Schwarze-negger what kind of woman he would like as a wife. "Dark-haired, pretty, intelligent, witty and very challenging," Schwarzenegger replied. "Otherwise I would walk all over her."[81] Another friend, Ben Weider, the brother of the businessman who had brought Schwarzenegger to America, recalls, "Arnold said at the beginning of his time in America that he was going to fulfill certain goals, one of which was to marry into a leading American family."[82] And in 1977, the same year the movie *Pumping Iron* was released, Schwarzenegger met the woman who was a perfect amalgam of the characteristics he had envisioned in an ideal mate.

With green eyes and a mane of dark hair, high cheekbones and a distinctive jaw, Maria Shriver is a striking woman. Though she was so lovely as a child that strangers had often stopped to remark on her exceptional beauty, she had not been raised to rely upon her looks. When people would comment on her beauty, her mother would tell her daughter, "Don't pay attention to that. It's your mind [that's important]."[83] Shriver took the lesson to heart, competing as if she were one of the boys with her four brothers. As an adult, she thrived in the rough-and-tumble world of television journalism where she initially was dismissed as a "rich little dilettante."[84] She has also written best-selling books, two for children and one a young adult's advice guide.

57

In addition, Shriver is a member of the Kennedy family. Often called America's royalty, the Kennedys' unrivaled prominence raised questions about whether love or political cunning led to the Schwarzenegger-Shriver match. Shriver's mother, Eunice Kennedy Shriver, is the sister of former president John F. Kennedy. Eunice Shriver founded the Special Olympics, the internationally known organization that hosts athletic competitions for people with mental retardation. Maria Shriver's father, Sargent Shriver, founded the Peace Corps, an organization that sends Americans to developing countries to help them in a variety of ways, and Head Start, a preschool program to help poor children. He worked in the administrations of both Presidents Kennedy and Lyndon B. Johnson before becoming an ambassador to France and a vice presidential candidate.

With tremendous wealth and good looks, the Kennedy family has long captured the public's fascination because of the almost mythic proportions of its achievements and tragedies. President John F. Kennedy, the youngest man and the first

A beautiful child, Maria Shriver matured into a striking and intelligent woman. She is pictured here between her parents in a family photo.

Pictured here in 1980, the articulate and strong-willed Maria Shriver embodied the traits that Arnold Schwarzenegger sought in a wife.

Roman Catholic to be elected president, was assassinated in 1963 before the end of his first term. Four and a half years later, his brother Robert Kennedy, who had served as attorney general before being elected as a U.S. senator from New York, was assassinated, too, while campaigning for the presidency. Another brother, Edward Kennedy, a longtime U.S. senator from Massachusetts, was at one time a front-runner among likely presidential contenders, but his chances effectively ended after he fled the scene of an infamous 1969 car accident that led to the death of a young woman in his car.

The Ultimate Outsider

Shriver was twenty-one, two months out of Georgetown University, when she met Schwarzenegger, then a thirty-year-old cult figure thanks to the popularity of *Pumping Iron*. They were introduced at a celebrity tennis tournament held annually in

Forest Hills, New York, to honor her late uncle. Schwarzenegger, who had sought an invitation to the event and like the rest
of the world was fascinated with the Kennedys, was a hit. A be-
ginner at tennis, he hammed up his lack of skills and, along with
his partner, the former football star Rosie Grier, lost to two ten-
year-olds.

"Next thing you know, he's in Hyannisport (the site of the
Kennedy family compound)," says Bobby Shriver, Maria's
brother. "That day. He didn't even go back to the hotel. Maria
said, 'Do you want to come up for the weekend? The plane is
leaving in two hours.' He said, 'Fine.'"[85] Once there, Schwarzenegger conversed in German with Shriver's grandmother, ma-
triarch Rose Kennedy. He burnished his reputation for blunt
speaking, telling Eunice Kennedy that her daughter had a great
behind, using a coarse term to describe that aspect of her
anatomy. Maria Shriver, who said she fell in love with Schwarzenegger immediately, recalls his remarks saying, "I don't know
how he gets away with that kind of thing, but my mother
laughed her head off."[86]

Shriver liked his sense of humor and his bold ambition, saying, "I was fascinated by his ability to say, 'I don't care what they
say, I know where I'm going.'"[87] She liked Schwarzenegger's
identity as an utter outsider with a life and persona far removed
from the family business of politics. She related to Schwarzenegger's legendary discipline, too. At the beginning of her television journalism career, when an agent insisted he would not
consider representing her until she shed both twenty-five
pounds and her nasal voice, Shriver did both.

From that beginning, a nine-year-long courtship began,
spanning two coasts and the meteoric rise of two careers. From
its inception, the romance puzzled many people because the
couple seemed opposite in fundamental respects. Everyone she
knew, Shriver says, assumed she was dating someone so different merely to rebel. "People would always say, 'Well why are
you with him?'" Shriver recalls. "And then when they met
Arnold, I never heard that again, and I think that they realized
how smart he was, how charming he was, how funny he is, and
I think people who knew me understood our connection."[88] She

Although some friends questioned Maria's attraction to Schwarzenegger, her mother Eunice Shriver (left) took an instant liking to him.

easily jokes about some reasons for her attraction to him, saying "Hello? Have you checked out the body? You think I'm blind, or what?"[89]

Political Differences

Perhaps the most glaring question about the match was the gulf in their political views. In the United States, two major political parties, the Democrats and Republicans, generally compete to win elections. Though political parties' philosophies evolve over the course of history, Democrats tend to support government's central role in helping to solve society's problems, while Republicans believe government's role, and its taxes, ought to be reduced in favor of more private-sector answers to problems. The Kennedy family is the unsurpassed standard bearer for the Democrats. Schwarzenegger is a Republican.

"Schwarzenegger knew he was a Republican in 1968," the year he immigrated, according to one interviewer. "To help him learn English, a friend translated the television speeches of presidential candidates. 'I like (Richard) Nixon,' Schwarzenegger told his friend."[90] That single sentence spoke volumes about the chasm between his political views and those of Shriver's family. In 1960 Republican candidate Richard M. Nixon narrowly lost his first bid for the presidency to Democrat John F. Kennedy.

In 1968—a year that witnessed both Robert Kennedy's assassination and Schwarzenegger's arrival in America—Nixon ran again and won. Schwarzenegger said hearing Democratic presidential candidate Hubert Humphrey speak that year reminded him of the socialism and limited opportunities he had left behind in Austria, while hearing Nixon speak, advocating free enterprise, reminded him of the opportunities America offered. Schwarzenegger's earliest experiences in the United States solidified his political outlook. Not long after he arrived, Schwarzenegger and weight lifter friend Franco Columbu had started a bricklaying business and mail-order bodybuilding course. Schwarzenegger was astonished at how easy starting the businesses had been, compared to the regulatory hurdles that would have been in place in Austria. "I said to Franco as we walked out of City Hall (with a business license), 'Can you believe this? They didn't ask anything. We didn't put up any money. We didn't have to have any banking proofs or any (college) degrees, any of these complications.'"[91]

In 1972 Nixon was reelected to the office by the largest margin in American history. His opponent was George McGovern, whose running mate that year happened to be Sargent Shriver. Sixteen-year-old Maria Shriver traveled with the press corps while on the campaign trail with her father. The experience proved to be the catalyst for her journalism career. At the time, her father's defeat so mortified her that she did not want to go to school the next day.

Common Interests

Over the years both Schwarzenegger and Shriver have made light of their political differences, stressing that they share core beliefs, even on political matters concerning family and women's issues. As she once joked to her uncle, the longtime U.S. senator Edward Kennedy, "Don't look at him as a Republican, look at him as the man I love. And if that doesn't work, look at him as someone who can squash you."[92] For all the outward differences, Shriver and Schwarzenegger insist they have much in common. Both like athletic pursuits, such as skiing; both share a wacky sense of humor; and both are enormously ambitious. As Shriver observes in her 2000 book, *Ten Things I Wish I'd Known —Before I Went Out into the Real World*, "He realized that I would be a handful as a wife. (And I would have had to have been deaf, blind, and incredibly stupid not to see that he was more than a handful himself.)"[93]

A Self-Made Man

From the beginning, Shriver found Schwarzenegger's confidence appealing. In the face of the Kennedys' wealth and accumulation of degrees from elite schools, Schwarzenegger held his own, though he came from a humble background and had relatively little formal education. (He obtained a bachelor's degree at age thirty-one from the University of Wisconsin–Superior by patching together correspondence courses and credits from a city college and university extension courses.)

In a motivational speech he gave decades after meeting the Shrivers and Kennedys, Schwarzenegger used the experience to dismiss the frequent complaints he says he hears from people who believe they are handicapped by their background.

> I could have said that. I could have said I couldn't compete when I met Maria and she invited me up to Hyannis Port to meet her family. I could have been intimidated, but instead I turned the situation around and used it to my advantage. I told myself "This is great! Here I am—meeting really smart people and political leaders who've dedicated their lives to public service.

What Maria Learned from Arnold

In her 2000 book *Ten Things I Wish I'd Known—Before I Went Out into the Real World*, Maria Shriver lists the top lessons life had offered her so far. Life Lesson Number Eight is entitled "Marriage Is a Hell of a Lot of Hard Work." In the chapter she notes that many people make a giant mistake by expecting a partner in marriage to do it all, to "make you happy, fix you, complete you, define you, make your life for you, make your life meaningful for you." Fortunately, she says, the man she eventually married disabused her of this notion before they exchanged their vows:

> After a while together, my future husband said to me, "Don't expect or rely on me to make you happy." Well, I thought, isn't his grasp of the English language adorable. He doesn't realize what he's saying. Who else is supposed to make me happy, if not him? But he was adamant. "You must be happy with yourself first. Be happy with your life separate from what the other person brings to the table." This was serious. He told me he'd be the icing on the cake, but that I shouldn't expect him to be the whole dessert. Now, that definitely wouldn't make a good lyric for a romantic love song, but I knew he was right.

Maria believes that a practical approach to marriage is responsible for the success of her relationship with Arnold.

I can learn from them!" And it turned out to be the smartest thing I ever did. Because not only did I learn a lot, I got a wife out of it, too![94]

Schwarzenegger adhered to his political convictions and his improbable career plan despite the Kennedy-Shriver family beliefs. Initially, he recalls, the Shrivers, like so many others, were skeptical of his lofty ambition to become a Hollywood superstar. "I told the Shrivers that I was going to be a number-one box office star some day, like Clint Eastwood. They said that was very, very lovely, but didn't I think I should have a fallback—like a nice Master's Degree in nutrition?"[95]

An Engagement

In 1985 Schwarzenegger's longtime friend Jim Lorimer, a partner in promoting bodybuilding competitions, offered his friend some advice. As the two men sat in a hot tub, Lorimer told his friend,

Arnold, you have just about everything a person could want. You don't have to work again ever if you don't want. But it's essential that you experience all of life's processes. One of the great, great pleasures is parenthood, marriage, grandchildren. You've been going with this woman (Shriver) eight years now. You've both got career challenges and pressures, but your love has continued to grow. So it's about time you thought about marrying her.[96]

Schwarzenegger apparently followed his friend's advice. He chose a dramatic setting for his proposal, asking Shriver to marry him as the two sat in a rowboat on the Thalersee, the lake where he had learned to swim as a boy. Eight weeks after his conversation with Schwarzenegger, Lorimer received a telegram from the couple announcing their engagement.

The Wedding

Schwarzenegger and Shriver wed on a cold and gloomy April 26, 1986, in the clapboard St. Francis Xavier Church in Hyannis, where Kennedys have attended Mass for generations. The event was a celebrity-studded affair, attended by a cross-section of the nation's political, media, sports, and pop culture elite, and recorded by, as one reporter cheekily observed, "seemingly half the photographers in America."[97]

Bodybuilder Franco Columbu was Schwarzenegger's best man. Caroline Kennedy, Shriver's cousin and the daughter of the late president Kennedy and Jacqueline Kennedy Onassis, was the

Although the weather is dismal and cold, Maria and Arnold are jubilant as they leave the church after their wedding ceremony in 1986.

maid of honor among the ten bridesmaids, dressed in a rainbow of colors. The television talk show star Oprah Winfrey, a friend of the bride's from their days at a Baltimore television station, read Elizabeth Barrett Browning's "How Do I Love Thee?" After saying their vows the couple walked back up the aisle to the Rogers and Hammerstein wedding march that had been written for the movie *The Sound of Music*, based on the story of a family in Austria on the brink of World War II. Shriver wore an elaborate Christian Dior–designed gown with an eleven-foot-long train. Schwarzenegger wore a cutaway tuxedo. A report notes that "Earlier Schwarzenegger [had] led his musclemen on a foray to Mr. Perry's Tux to fit them out in cutaways and to everyone's amazement [given their huge physiques], succeeded."[98]

The Reception

Following the seventy-five-minute Roman Catholic Mass, guests attended the lavish reception, where the bride, who had broken two toes earlier, slipped into white tennis shoes. The wedding cake, a replica of the one that had been served at the wedding of the bride's parents, stood seven feet tall and weighed more than four hundred pounds. The groom gave his new in-laws a silk screen portrait of his bride created by a wedding guest, the pop artist Andy Warhol. "I'm not really taking her away, because I am giving this to you so you will always have her,"[99] he told them.

Schwarzenegger made one other memorable speech at the reception, one that haunted him for decades. The groom toasted a controversial friend, Kurt Waldheim, a former secretary general of the United Nations who was running for president of Austria and was accused of lying about his Nazi past. Schwarzenegger later apologized for the remarks, saying, "It was a mistake."[100]

A Family

For many years the marriage continued as their courtship had, with Shriver pursuing her journalism career, Schwarzenegger pursuing his movies, and the two of them frequently on opposite coasts. Shriver, who had begun her career as a newswriter and producer at television stations in Philadelphia and Baltimore, had become coanchor of the failing *CBS Morning News*.

She was fired from CBS but landed at NBC, where she refash-
ioned her career. There she anchored a Sunday news show and
a children's news hour, and conducted award-winning, high-
profile interviews and feature news pieces. She also went on to
write three books, two of them for children: *What's Heaven?* is
Shriver's answer to her daughters' questions about the death of
their great-grandmother, Rose Kennedy. *What's Wrong With
Timmy?* reflects the Kennedy family's long-standing concern for
people such as Shriver's aunt, Rosemary Kennedy, who is men-
tally retarded.

Though both Shriver and Schwarzenegger continued to pur-
sue their careers, the birth of the couple's four children changed
their focus toward family and ended their bicoastal commute.
Katherine was born on December 13, 1989; Christina, on July
23, 1991; Patrick, on September 18, 1993; and Christopher, on
September 27, 1997. As Schwarzenegger once said, "I never saw
myself as a guy that could settle down. I was always very deroga-
tory about the station wagons that people used in the '60s and
'70s, with the dog and the cat and the kids screaming—and now
I'm driving around with the dogs, the puppies, the kids screaming in the back, the wife in the front seat, trying to calm everyone down."[101]

Shriver drastically cut back on her work hours and, she said,
on other career opportunities. (Once, she famously canceled a
scheduled interview with Cuban president Fidel Castro because
it conflicted with her older daughter's first day of preschool, and
the mercurial Castro, reportedly charmed by her dedication to
her children, agreed to reschedule.) Though Schwarzenegger
did not follow suit, he made other changes in an attempt to accommodate his family, flying home most weekends and making
it a point not to miss important family occasions or birthdays.

Though the family lives in opulence most people can only
imagine—with mansions in Brentwood and Pacific Palisades in
Southern California and a vacation home in Sun Valley, Idaho
—the couple are trying to give their children a "normal" life,
and friends say their children do not fit the stereotype of the
spoiled celebrity child. Schwarzenegger insists that his children
do their own laundry and rinse their dishes, for instance, and

Heart Surgery

In 1997, at age forty-nine, Arnold Schwarzenegger underwent surgery to replace a part of the heart called a valve. Valves control the blood flow through the heart. Schwarzenegger's defective valve was replaced with a healthy, donated human one.

The operation fueled speculation about whether Schwarzenegger's use of steroids had been more extensive than he had previously acknowledged. Steroid use can lead to heart disease. However, doctors said Schwarzenegger had been born with the defective valve.

Schwarzenegger chose to have the surgery while he remained in good health. "Over the years, the valve would have deteriorated and would have had to be replaced," Vaughn Starnes, the chief of cardiothoracic surgery who led the surgical team, said in a hospital press release.

In an interview with E! Online, a celebrity Internet site, Schwarzenegger said the heart surgery had not led to any major changes in his life. Though he scaled back somewhat on weightlifting, which he still does daily, the actor said he was trying to live his life as if the surgery had never happened:

> I come from denial. If I have something wrong, it doesn't exist. With the surgery, no one was allowed to talk about it. I didn't tell anyone I was going to do it—not even my wife—until a week before. I didn't want to talk about it, because if I talk about it, then I'm having heart surgery. In my mind, maybe I'm having a tooth removed. . . . I told Maria I never want to talk about this again. It just didn't exist.

Shriver drives in carpools to take the children to their private schools. Reportedly, the children are not allowed to watch television on schooldays, and the telephone is unplugged between 4 P.M. and 8 P.M. every weekday to allow them to focus on homework and family dinner. Weekends are filled with the children's activities and Catholic Mass.

"They complain about their laundry a lot," Shriver says. "But Arnold was really adamant that the kids be responsible for themselves and to learn how to take care of themselves and to clean their own rooms, do their own laundry, [and] clean the table."[102]

A family friend, Roberta Hollander, a producer in the *CBS News* Los Angeles bureau, says, "I have watched Maria and Arnold grow their children for almost 14 years now, and it has been a real eye opener. It's a lesson for all of us in everything that a loving family should be."[103]

Though Schwarzenegger has admitted to past inappropriate behavior with women, and questions have surrounded him about his fidelity to his wife, Shriver has consistently portrayed him as a loving husband. "He tells me all the time . . . how extraordinary I am, how beautiful I am, how much he loves me. Every day he brings me coffee in the morning and tells me that he loves me,"[104] Shriver says.

New Roles

The start of his own family and the influence of his extended Shriver family have had a powerful influence on Schwarzenegger's charitable pursuits. Before he met his wife and her family, he claims in various interviews, he thought only of "me, me, me."[105] He tells how exposure to the Shrivers' and Kennedys' passion for public service changed him:

> They think so much about serving the public, about social work and being involved in politics and charitable activi-

Schwarzenegger plays with a competitor at the 2001 Special Olympics in China. He credits the Shrivers and the Kennedys with awakening his interest in social work and charitable causes.

ties. So much of their dialogue at home deals with "What can we do for others?" and eventually this has an effect on you. Sports are a very selfish activity because you think only about yourself. Even in team sports you are trying to make that score, and thinking about yourself as an athlete. So it was ideal for me to be exposed to that other side where no one talks about "me," they talk about you.[106]

Once, Schwarzenegger says, he spoke to his father-in-law about the thrill he had experienced when helping children with mental retardation try to bench-press weights. Sargent Shriver insightfully suggested: "Break that mirror in front of you—that mirror that only lets you look at yourself. Break it, so you can look beyond! You'll see the rest of the world. You'll see people who need your help!"[107] It was a powerful message for a man whose accomplishments had been so tied to an image in a mirror.

Schwarzenegger responded to that message by taking on a variety of children's causes. Since 1979 he has traveled the world fund-raising and volunteering as the international weight training coach for the Special Olympics, the organization founded in 1968 by his mother-in-law. In 1991 Schwarzenegger founded his own children's charity, the Inner-City Games, a nonprofit organization that seeks to provide poor children living in crime-ridden urban areas free opportunities to participate in sports, educational, and cultural programs. The organization, operating in more than a dozen cities across the nation, aims to offset the effects of poverty and the lure of gangs by offering children ways to build strong bodies and agile minds—offering, for instance, athletic pursuits and classes in chess.

Twice in his career, Schwarzenegger has sought to combine children's causes and politics. In 1990 Republican president George H.W. Bush named Schwarzenegger chairman of the President's Council on Physical Fitness and Sports. Schwarzenegger held the job for two years and became one of the nation's most high-profile activists, traveling to fifty states to promote daily, quality physical education in the nation's schools.

In 2002 he headed a California campaign to promote expansion of the state's before-and-after-school programs for children.

The measure, Proposition 49, the After School Education and Safety Program Act of 2002, promised to expand tutoring, art, sports, and computer classes for children, and backers said it would reduce the likelihood of youths becoming involved in gang and crime activities after school. "My goal is to create a safe, educationally enriching and fun after school environment at all of California's public elementary and middle schools," Schwarzenegger said. "Providing a supervised and structured after school haven for our most vulnerable youth not only protects our school children, it keeps our neighborhoods safe."[108] Detractors called the measure irresponsible, because it did not provide for a new source of money to pay for its programs. "The money would have to come from somewhere, very possibly from health care or social services that kids need, too," the *Sacramento Bee* observed. "The state is already in terrible financial shape, and Proposition 49 would just dig a deeper hole."[109]

In November 2002 the measure passed handily, but a year later, no money for the programs had materialized. Years-long delays were forecast, the result of the California government's budget crisis and provisions stipulating that certain state fiscal conditions had to be met before the measure would begin.

Most political observers viewed Schwarzenegger's role in Proposition 49 as a prelude to a run for governor four years later. They openly wondered whether Schwarzenegger was up to the task. "Arnold Schwarzenegger has faced all kinds of nemeses in his movie career. He has been shot, stabbed, run over, burned, crushed, melted and had his memory erased by Martian forces. He has even been impregnated," a veteran political reporter for the *Los Angeles Times* observed that year. He went on to suggest that even these adversaries and adversities could pale in the face of the world of California politics, "a place where enemies stoke an adversarial press corps, where reporters wear their skepticism proudly, and where character is not a role but the measure of a person to be publicly, minutely scrutinized."[110]

As it happened, observers did not have to wait four years to witness how Schwarzenegger would fare in the cutthroat world of California politics. Thanks to a bizarre and unprecedented election, Schwarzenegger answered that question within a year.

Chapter 5

Governor Schwarzenegger

On the afternoon of August 6, 2003, Arnold Schwarzenegger masterminded a spectacularly dramatic entrance into the world of politics. Schwarzenegger arrived at the Burbank, California, studios for the taping of the *Tonight Show*, the late-night television talk show starring Jay Leno, to stage what would become one of the boldest and most surprising stunts in the annals of political theater. Everyone—even his own political adviser—expected him to opt out of the race for governor of California. To bolster the illusion that he planned to sit out the race, Schwarzenegger's chief political guru, George Gorton, stood backstage holding a news release that explained the reasons behind the actor's decision not to run.

But before a whooping audience at the studio taping that afternoon, and before a whopping television audience that night, one of the largest of the year for the *Tonight Show*, Schwarzenegger dropped his bombshell. He announced that he would run for his first public office: governor of California, the nation's most populous and trendsetting state. As Gorton later said, "It was a masterstroke in political theater."[111]

That curtain-raiser surprised political analysts, but it was a vintage Schwarzenegger move. To those who had closely followed his bodybuilding career, the scene merely reprised another surprise entrance he had plotted decades earlier for another contest, the competition for the Mr. Olympia crown of 1980. In that contest, held five years after the six-time champion

bodybuilder had retired from professional competition,
Schwarzenegger flew to Sydney, Australia, ostensibly to provide
color commentary for CBS television coverage of the event. Instead, he abruptly entered the competition, a shrewd move that
angered key competitors and caught them off guard. With that,
he set the stage for his seventh Mr. Olympia crown, a victory so
controversial that Schwarzenegger, used to the adoration of
bodybuilding audiences, received boos because many in the audience did not think he deserved to win.

The gambit that had led to his final Mr. Olympia title worked
for him twenty-three years later when he stepped into the rough-
and-tumble arena of California politics. Dan Walters, a veteran
political columnist for the *Sacramento Bee*, thought the move revealed the very essence of Schwarzenegger, the man: "The very
beginnings of the Schwarzenegger campaign hinted both at his
penchant for games (he kept a chessboard in his dressing room)

*In a surprise move on August 6, 2003, Schwarzenegger announces his
candidacy for governor of California on Jay Leno's* Tonight Show.

and his highly focused, almost ruthless, will to dominate whatever venue he occupies—bodybuilding, Hollywood and now politics."[112]

An Unusual Election for an Unusual Candidate

Schwarzenegger's candidacy was unprecedented, but then, so was the election itself, a circuslike political spectacle to people watching from other parts of the nation and the globe. But the absurdities belied its serious stakes. And in short, it was the perfect springboard for the idiosyncratic Schwarzenegger whose timing, as usual, proved impeccable.

For the first time in the state's 153-year history, voters in California were poised to remove a sitting governor from office. Millions of Californians signed a petition seeking to recall Governor Gray Davis, a Democrat who had been elected to his second term just months earlier, in November 2002. The recall petition accused Davis of grossly mismanaging the state. It reads, in part, "California should not have to be known as the state with poor schools, traffic jams, outrageous utility bills, and huge debts."[113]

Though the recall effort initially was viewed as a far-fetched political stunt, it tapped the latent anger of California voters who had accumulated a long list of grievances. The state was spending more money than it was taking in, so much so that its estimated $38 billion shortfall was larger than the entire budget of any other state. Though the economy nationwide had stalled, in California events bore a special drama. The economy had plummeted after a time of heady excess. Only a few years earlier California's innovative Silicon Valley had spawned the "dot-com" revolution and given rise to a class of multimillionaires under the age of thirty. Though California was the most technologically advanced state in the nation, it was struggling with many problems. It had difficulty keeping its lights on during an electricity crisis under a plan devised to lower electricity costs. The state's public schools, once a point of pride, were crumbling and held in ill regard. Voters seethed over what they considered to be excessive taxes and put the blame on the shoulders of their aloof governor, Gray Davis, a Democrat. In short, the "Golden State," as California calls itself, seemed tarnished. John Pitney, government professor at Claremont McKenna College and former Republican Party strategist, explains:

> We used to be the state that everybody looked up to, and now we're the state that everybody looks down on. There is a gap between the California myth and the real California. Everybody in California is aware of the state's reputation, the one in the theme song of the old television series, *The Beverly Hillbillies*, with "swimming pools and movie stars." Then we drive on pitted roads to send our children to inadequate schools. I think Schwarzenegger accurately diagnosed the California electorate in that we're pretty dissatisfied.[114]

Schwarzenegger and California seemed to be an ideal match in many respects. Schwarzenegger's Hollywood glamour and compelling rags-to-riches immigrant tale gave him a larger-than-life quality. This seemed perfectly suited to a state where the public policy problems had grown to enormous proportions, the political equivalent of an improbable *Terminator* plot. In fact, as followers of Schwarzenegger's movie career knew, as dire as the political challenges seemed, they were modest compared to the life-threatening hurdles his heroic cyborgs in "T2" and "T3" handle with such dispatch. Never mind that those inspiring feats are works of illusion and fiction.

"The reason an outsider or celebrity has so much appeal is because the problems seem larger than life," explains Mark Baldassare, director of the Public Policy Institute of California, a nonpartisan research group. "That leads people to think that ordinary politicians are not relevant in this situation."[115]

A Sixty-Three-Day Campaign

Nine weeks after his bold political opening at age fifty-six, Schwarzenegger won the audition for the most ambitious role of his life in an election the likes of which the nation had never witnessed before. The star, whose political record was so scant it extended for only the sixty-three days of his campaign, triumphed over a sitting governor, Gray Davis, who had twice been elected to the office and had worked in politics for three decades. Not only

Despite his lack of political experience, Schwarzenegger connected with Californians during his brief sixty-three-day campaign for governor.

did Republican Schwarzenegger win the state's top elected post at a time when all the statewide offices were held by the rival political party, the Democrats, he clearly outshone everyone in the bizarre field of 135 candidates seeking the office. The threshold to seek office was surprisingly low; anyone willing to pay a thirty-five-hundred-dollar filing fee and gather sixty-five signatures on a petition was eligible. As a result the race for a replacement governor drew so many candidates that the list of names on the ballot extended for seven pages. Aspirants to the office included serious candidates such as experienced elected officials and a former major league baseball commissioner, and seriously strange candidates such as the publisher of a pornographic magazine, an X-rated movie star, a billboard model, a sumo wrestler, a faded star from a defunct television sitcom, and a comedian whose trademark gag is smashing watermelons.

Schwarzenegger was not the first Hollywood figure to enter politics, but his candidacy eclipsed his predecessors' examples both for its impatience and its ambition. Ronald Reagan had been a B-grade movie actor before becoming governor of California and president of the United States, but before seeking office he had toiled in the conservative political movement for years. Sonny Bono, the comic sidekick to his glamorous former wife, the singer Cher, was elected mayor of Palm Springs and as a U.S. congressman after his entertainment career waned. Clint Eastwood, another celebrated tough-guy actor still on the big screen, was elected mayor of Carmel, California. But Schwarzenegger was not seeking a ceremonial post as mayor or to be merely one of 435 members of the U.S. House of Representatives.

That the world-famous action hero was not content to wait until his movie career was over was obvious. Indeed, the same summer he appeared on the national stage as a candidate seeking office, he reprised his cyborg role in *Terminator 3: Rise of the Machines*, which opened just thirty-seven days before he announced he would run for governor.

Characteristically, Schwarzenegger had set his political ambitions sky high—aiming to take the helm of California, a state that was home to one of every eight Americans, boasted an economy larger than all but four nations, and served as the nation's leading political laboratory. His decision to aim immediately for one of the nation's most prominent political perches recalled the same impatient ambition he had displayed at age nineteen when he first sought the mighty Mr. Universe crown—and won it a year later.

Name, Money, and Theatrics

Schwarzenegger adroitly stepped into the recall fray with the time-tested elixir of modern politics: name recognition and money. He needed to run only on his first name, a point underscored by his campaign signs, which said, simply, "Join Arnold." His signature movie titles (*Total Recall, Running Man*), characters (the Terminator), and lines ("Hasta la vista, baby") morphed into campaign slogans. His movie career inspired unlimited campaign puns, which proved so pervasive that at one point a Fox News Channel executive ordered his television staff to avoid them. But with no one else following suit, the puns proliferated, with entrepreneurs seizing on the moment to hawk T-shirts, bumper stickers, and mouse pads sporting the words, "Governator," "Conan the Republican," and "Vote for me if you want to live." A toy maker sold a twelve-inch "Governator" action-figure doll that talked, droning with the actor's trademark deadpan delivery, "I will go to Sacramento and I will clean house . . . trust me, I'll be back."[116]

Money is the lifeblood of political campaigns because it buys the television, radio, and printed advertisements candidates use to get their message to voters. Schwarzenegger promised to use his own money to get elected. He did. He spent $6.5 million of his own money, a figure that made him by far the top spender in the race. In addition, he took out $2.5 million in bank loans to help pay for the campaign. At the beginning of the race he vowed not to take anyone else's money. That way, he said, he would not be beholden to the various special interests competing to advance their agendas in the state's political system. But soon Schwarzenegger backed away from that pledge and raised $12 million from outside sources.

The theatricality of both his bodybuilding and movie careers gave Schwarzenegger a flair for the dramatic that he used on the campaign trail. His campaign adopted a theme song, the 1984 throbbing heavy metal anthem "We're Not Going to Take It" by the band Twisted Sister, and the group appeared with him on the campaign. Well versed in the power of special effects, Schwarzenegger used a Hollywood-like stunt to dramatize his pledge to roll back a recent tripling of the state's vehicle licensing tax. "In the movies, if I played a character and I didn't like something, you know what I did? I destroyed it," Schwarzenegger said to a crowd in Costa Mesa. "I brought some of my Hollywood pals here so I can show you exactly what we are going to do to the car tax."[117] At that moment a wrecking ball fell on a car that crumpled in a spray of broken glass and twisted metal, and the audience roared.

Schwarzenegger employed other Hollywood tools in his campaign, too. One of them was the confidentiality agreement. To protect his privacy, members of his campaign staff were required to sign a five-page agreement that was essentially an extensive list of prohibitions. They were forbidden to reveal any information about Schwarzenegger, his family, friends, associates,

Rocky Contemplates President Conan

In the 1993 movie, *Demolition Man*, actor Sylvester Stallone plays a cop who has been cryogenically frozen and then thawed in the year 2032. When another character, played by actress Sandra Bullock, updates Stallone's character on the state of world affairs, she mentions the Schwarzenegger Library.

"Hold it," a shocked Stallone says. "The Schwarzenegger Library?"

The Schwarzenegger Presidential Library, Bullock's character explains, asking, "Wasn't he an actor?"

Stallone replies, "Stop. He was president?"

Bullock begins to go on about how Schwarzenegger's popularity led to the passage of an amendment repealing a provision in the Constitution requiring that anyone seeking the presidency be born in the United States. But Stallone interrupts her with a groan, saying, "I don't want to know."

Within ten years, one issue raised in the movie scene had managed to transcend Hollywood fiction and move onto the national political stage. In 2003 Orrin Hatch, a U.S. senator, introduced an amendment

to make an immigrant eligible for the presidency after twenty years of citizenship. Though the Utah Republican said he did not have anyone in particular in mind when he sponsored the legislation, his proposal was dubbed the Arnold Amendment. Hatch and Schwarzenegger are friends, and 2003 happened to be the twentieth anniversary of Schwarzenegger's citizenship.

In Demolition Man, *Sylvester Stallone's character contemplates an Arnold Schwarzenegger presidency.*

and employees—either during or after the campaign. They were also barred from taking photographs, movies, videos, or drawing sketches of Schwarzenegger, his family, friends, associates, and employees. "Such nondisclosure agreements are standard in the movie industry, but unusual in political campaigns,"[118] the *Los Angeles Times* noted. Schwarzenegger's strategists said the agreements were necessary because of the candidate's celebrity. But Schwarzenegger was criticized for the practice, accused of being hypocritical by calling for more open government yet using practices to make his campaign more secretive. "What if [former president] Lyndon Johnson had required his staff to sign confidentiality agreements?" author Richard Blow asks in a *New York Times* column that relates the chilling effect such agreements had had in his efforts to publish his book about John F. Kennedy Jr. "How much valuable information would be lost to history? . . . Confidentialty agreements allow Mr. Schwarzenegger to enter the public arena with very little of the risk that every other noncelebrity politician must live with: that the public will learn unfortunate truths about him."[119]

Not Politics as Usual

From the beginning, Schwarzenegger sought to portray himself as an agent of change, an outsider who intended to govern by using the same skills that had taken him to the pinnacles of success and power in all his previous life's pursuits. He spoke nostalgically of his arrival in California and the changes that had hurt the state:

> When I first came to California 35 years ago, California was a place of dreams. This great state said to the people everywhere: Come here, work hard, play by the rules, and your dreams can come true. But today, the dream— and the optimism that California represented to this nation and the world—has been shattered. I believe we can restore that optimism and the dreams that were once fulfilled here. Our people are good people—they work hard, they're paying their taxes, they're raising their families, and they're doing everything they can to provide their children with the tools to succeed. We have everything we need here in California—except leadership. . . . I am running for governor to lead a movement for change and give California back its future.[120]

It mattered not that in many key respects the so-called golden age of California was more a product of myth than reality.

The celebrity candidate quickly found himself with problems run-of-the-mill politicians could only envy. Though backers of candidates for office typically work feverishly behind the scenes to ensure attendance at their rallies, Schwarzenegger was mobbed to such a degree that his handlers instead worried about crowd control. After people were nearly trampled by the mob at one of his first campaign stops in Huntington Beach, the central question for future public events, improbably enough, became: "'How many bicycle racks do you have?' The metal racks were used to provide a barrier over which the candidate could shake hands without being trampled by eager fans."[121]

Schwarzenegger's media entourage was also a striking departure from the traditional pack of reporters who cover gubernatorial races. The unheard of mix of reporters on the Schwarzenegger campaign trail included representatives from Austria, China, France, Japan, Italy, Russia, *Entertainment Tonight*, and Ironmanmagazine.com, among others. Television news, usually berated for being practically devoid of meaningful political coverage, could not get enough of Schwarzenegger. Through the Friday before election day, one analysis found "network news shows devoted 71 minutes to stories specifically about Schwarzenegger—twice as much time as they've devoted to the 10 Democratic candidates for president combined and 75 percent more than they devoted to all the gubernatorial races in the country combined in 2002."[122]

Though Schwarzenegger burnished his reputation as a canny businessman who had shrewdly invested his millions in real estate, his campaign rested largely on his celebrity. His prominence, and the tenor of the times, allowed him to twin celebrity and politics to an unprecedented degree. For instance, he deliberately avoided traditional political reporters who wanted budgetary figures and other details that would support his ambitious campaign promises. "The public doesn't care about figures," he said. "They have heard figures for the last five years. . . . What the people want to hear is are you willing to make the changes? Are you tough enough to go in there and provide leadership?"[123]

Instead, he waged his campaign in high-profile venues, hobnobbing with CNN's Larry King and national radio shock jock, Howard Stern. He and his wife, Maria Shriver, appeared on the season opener of a national show hosted by longtime friend Oprah

Winfrey. The interview did not touch on policy matters, its chief revelations being about Schwarzenegger's insistence on having his children do their own laundry, and his habit of bringing his wife coffee every morning. When he repeated a graphic remark about his "crazy days" promoting bodybuilding, comparing

Arnold the Car Salesman

The Hummer is Arnold Schwarzenegger on wheels. The vehicle is over-sized, attention getting, and sturdy as a tank. Schwarzenegger played a pivotal role in bringing the Hummer to the American public. The in-spiration for the Hummer was a military vehicle, the High Mobility Multipurpose Wheeled Vehicle. Soldiers called it the Humvee for short. Schwarzenegger first saw a Humvee while in Oregon shooting a movie, and he was so taken with the vehicle that he stopped soldiers to ask where he could get one. He flew to the factory in South Bend, Indiana, to persuade AM General to make a version for the public, and in 1992 he bought the first two Hummers to roll off the assembly line.

On his Internet site, in response to a fan's question, Schwarzenegger tries to explain the appeal the car held for him: "It's like love when you meet that girl, you just know. It was like that with the Hummer. I'd been looking for a car like that all my life." At the 2002 New York City debut of the smaller Hummer, the H2, Schwarzenegger admiringly stroked the car and said, "Look at those deltoids! Look at those calves!"

In 2003 the Hummer sold for $105,000, the same price as a typical family home in Dayton, Ohio, that year. The Hummer at that time was both the most popular and the most vilified vehicle on the road. In April 2003 the *New York Times* called the car one of the hottest-selling vehicles in the nation—conveying wealth, indestructibility, and, in some circles, patriotism, because of its military style and history. At the same time, the Hummer drew enormous criticism because of its ex-tremely low gas mileage, said to be eight to twelve miles per gallon, roughly half the average fuel efficiency level the government required manufacturers of light trucks to meet. The Sierra Club, a national en-vironmental group, considered the Hummer such an extreme example of waste and pollution that it created an Internet website specifically to satirize the car: hummerdinger.com.

The car is so identified with Schwarzenegger that it became a political issue during his campaign for governor. Environmentalists said Schwar-zenegger's vehicles (then five Hummers and two H2s) raised questions about his commitment to environmental causes. Schwarzenegger, who insists he supports environmental causes, responded by vowing to refit his Hummer to run on environmentally friendly fuel, hydrogen instead of gasoline.

pumping iron to sexual gratification, his horrified wife pressed her palm over his mouth and reminded him, "My mother is watching this show!"[124]

Missteps That Did Not Matter

Schwarzenegger, who had been viewed as the object of perfection in his bodybuilding career, did not wage a perfect campaign, but his victory made his mistakes fade. In the campaign's early days, Schwarzenegger had to explain why, despite his immigrant background, he supported a proposed California measure to bar government services, including health care and education, to illegal immigrants. He had to explain why he had such a spotty voting record, failing to vote in thirteen of the previous twenty elections. He had to explain why he differed with the views of his economic adviser, Warren Buffett, the world's second-richest man, who had criticized a wildly popular California law limiting the amount of taxes homeowners pay.

Early on in the campaign, Schwarzenegger also had to answer questions that stemmed from the outrageous image he portrayed and cultivated during his bodybuilding career. In an extensive interview in 1977 with a pornographic magazine called *Oui*, for instance, the twenty-nine-year-old Schwarzenegger made lewd and graphic remarks about his sexual practices and attitudes toward women and admitted to using illegal drugs. Questioned on the campaign trail about the article, Schwarzenegger gave a series of varying responses, first saying, "I never lived my life to be a politician. . . . Obviously, I've made statements that are ludicrous and crazy and outrageous and all those things, because that's the way I always was."[125] He later said he had no memory of the remarks. Even later, he said he had concocted the stories to boost the outrageous image he was trying to cultivate for himself and the sport of bodybuilding.

Nothing—not the pictures of him posing nude or with bare-breasted women sitting on his shoulders, not scenes of him smoking marijuana in *Pumping Iron*, not accusations of boorish and demeaning behavior toward women—diluted his appeal. On the campaign trail, he exuded his characteristic confidence and charm, magnetism and quick wits. When someone in Long

Neither Schwarzenegger's campaign missteps nor his controversial past affected his appeal to California's fascinated electorate.

Beach hit him with an egg at a campaign appearance, he reacted with a joke: "This guy owes me bacon now."[126] He joked that to punish Buffett, his seventy-three-year-old investment guru, for his unpopular criticism of California's property tax law, he would make the man do five hundred sit-ups.

His inexperience in politics did not seem to matter to voters who instead seemed to embrace it as a breath of fresh air. After his first news conference with reporters, seasoned *Los Angeles Times* political columnist George Skelton wrote, "Look, it's obvious that Schwarzenegger doesn't know beans about how state government works—how the money flows in and where it goes. But voters already believe him—as they did Ronald Reagan 37 years ago—when he tells them the government isn't working very well."[127]

A Vivid Contrast

The contrast between Schwarzenegger and his key competitors could not have been more striking. Gray Davis was so infamously bland and aloof that people complained that his first name perfectly described his personality. Cruz Bustamante, the Democratic lieutenant governor who led Schwarzenegger in the polls until the campaign's final two weeks, was described as having "all the charisma of a bowl of oatmeal."[128]

Schwarzenegger trailed Bustamante in polls for much of a campaign so odd that at one point even the date of the election itself was an open question as federal judges disagreed over when it ought to be held. But September 24 proved a turning point. With two weeks to go before election day, Schwarzenegger appeared in a debate among the top five replacement candidates for governor. The televised event, the lone debate in which Schwarzenegger had agreed to participate, was ridiculed for being too easy because the candidates were provided the questions in advance. *Tonight Show* host Jay Leno quipped, "It's like Jeopardy for dumb people."[129]

Though most Schwarzenegger aides felt his performance was only so-so, "a B minus,"[130] one senior aide said, the novice candi-

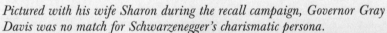

Pictured with his wife Sharon during the recall campaign, Governor Gray Davis was no match for Schwarzenegger's charismatic persona.

date benefited from the public's exceedingly low expectations. "His aides said that evening that all he needed to do was string a noun, a verb and a few statistics together to address any lingering concerns about his competence and cement his victory," a *New York Times* reporter later observed. "The actor did more than that, reciting the lines a joke writer had written for him."[131]

With that, Schwarzenegger surged ahead in polls and so did support for the recall, which had been losing momentum. Six days before the October 7 election, Schwarzenegger, brimming with confidence, delivered a symbolic speech from the same Sacramento auditorium where Davis had been sworn in as governor less than a year before. There he announced a ten-point agenda for his first one hundred days in office as if his victory were assured. Davis accused Schwarzenegger of "measuring the curtains in the offices of the capitol"[132] before the election.

Last-Minute Accusations

The most potentially damaging threats to his candidacy surfaced the very next day. On October 2 the *Los Angeles Times* published a long front-page article in which six women accused Schwarzenegger of sexually humiliating and mistreating them. Over the next several days more women came forward, bringing the total number to sixteen, eleven of whom were named in the article.

Schwarzenegger, who was just kicking off a statewide bus tour, spoke to supporters in San Diego about the accusations, saying, "I have behaved badly sometimes. Yes it is true that I was on rowdy movie sets and I have done things that were not right which I thought then was playful but now I recognize that I have offended people. And to those people that I have offended, I want to say to them I am deeply sorry about that."[133]

Maria Shriver, who had become a key figure in the campaign even before the allegations were published, took on an even more vital role. In public, she held his hand and kissed him, essentially saying with her gestures what she told a friend privately: "You know, as far as I'm concerned, everyone can listen to the *L.A. Times,* or they can listen to me."[134] Her role reminded many political observers of the critical one Hillary Rodham Clinton had played in confronting accusations about the sexual conduct of her husband, Bill Clinton, in his first campaign for president.

In the end, the *Los Angeles Times* suffered rather than Schwarzenegger. More than one thousand people canceled subscriptions, and the newspaper was accused of conspiring with the Democrats to defeat the Republican front-runner. In an extraordinary article published the Sunday after Schwarzenegger's victory, John S. Carroll, the newspaper's editor, wrote a vigorous defense of the paper's investigation, calling the stories "solid as Gibraltar" and noting that the facts in them had never been seriously challenged. "Better, I say, to be surprised by your newspaper in October than to learn in November that your newspaper has betrayed you by withholding the truth,"[135] Carroll wrote.

In her interview with Schwarzenegger and Shriver, Oprah Winfrey had said the candidate seemed to be Teflon coated. She was referring to his quick wits in handling the egging he took on the campaign trail, but it also proved true in other respects. No one seemed to mind that he had reneged on his promise to turn away donations, instead raising more money than any other candidate for the office. A last-minute charge, that as a young man Schwarzenegger had admired Adolf Hitler, disintegrated. Schwarzenegger himself vigorously denied the charge; years earlier he had donated millions of dollars to the Simon Wiesenthal Center, a Jewish organization in Los Angeles that works to preserve the memory of the Holocaust.

An Election Victory

On Tuesday, October 7, 2003, voters swept Schwarzenegger into office. By a margin of 55 percent to 45 percent, California passed the history-making recall. Schwarzenegger won 49 percent of the total votes for all the possible replacements, winning both more votes and a slightly higher percentage of the vote than Davis had garnered the previous year. His closest competitor, Cruz Bustamante, the Democrat lieutenant governor, trailed far behind with 32 percent.

That night, a jubilant Schwarzenegger, who had invested millions of his personal fortune—more than anyone else in the race—stood on a podium at the confetti-strewn Century Plaza

Hotel in Los Angeles, in a politically surreal tableau. Some of the nation's most famous Democrats stood with him—his wife's family members, including the sister of the late John F. Kennedy, Eunice Kennedy Shriver, who had campaigned for her son-in-law.

He thanked his wife first, saying, "I know how many votes I got today because of you."[136] He went on to thank the people of California, emphasizing that he wanted to be the people's governor:

> From the time I came over to this country, you opened your arms to me, you received me, you've given me opportunities, endless amounts of opportunities. Everything that I have is because of California. I came here with absolutely nothing and California has given me absolutely everything. And today California has given me the greatest gift of all. You've given me your trust by voting for me. . . . And let me tell you something. I will do everything I can to live up to that trust. I will not fail you. I will not disappoint you. And I will not let you down.[137]

Arnold and Maria savor his political triumph with her parents, Sargent and Eunice Shriver, as Arnold is inaugurated as the governor of California.

Schwarzenegger and his family arrive for his swearing-in ceremony as governor. Many people believe that the governorship is only the first step toward greater political ambitions.

Interpreting the Victory

From the campaign's beginning, and more feverishly after its end, people pondered the meaning of Schwarzenegger's appeal. "People want government to move more with the swiftness and the gratification of entertainment,"[138] opines Kevin Starr, the state's librarian and author of six California history books. That wish, he observes, is perfectly in keeping with a society that follows the news of the day through *West Wing*, a television series about White House politics, and gets its legal knowledge from *Law & Order*, a television crime drama. In Schwarzenegger's case, to make life imitate art completely, actor Rob Lowe, a former *West Wing* cast member, had served as a high-profile Arnold supporter.

Schwarzenegger's successful campaign, Starr says, had even turned an old saying of politics on its head: "Politics were once said to be show business for ugly people. Now we have to say that show business is politics for good-looking people. Successful politicians are going to come in all shapes, colors, creeds and body types. It doesn't mean that everybody has to be a Schwarzenegger, but candidates will have to seek this personal connection."[139]

What Is Next?

Even before his victory, seasoned Schwarzenegger observers wondered whether the California governor's office might prove to be merely another Schwarzenegger stepping-stone. In the summer of 2003, Republican senator Orrin Hatch of Utah introduced a resolution to amend the U.S. Constitution to allow foreign-born citizens who have lived here for at least twenty years to ascend to the presidency. "If Arnold Schwarzenegger turns out to be the greatest governor of California, which I hope he will, if he turns out to be a tremendous leader and he proved to everybody in this country that he's totally dedicated to this country as an American, we would be wrong not to give him that opportunity,"[140] Hatch said.

And those who know the bodybuilder-turned-actor-turned-politician say there is no question that Schwarzenegger, with his boundless ambition and relentless drive, would seek the opportunity. It would only be following "the Master Plan" he drafted for himself as a young boy in Austria. He has followed that life's blueprint, down to its smallest details, every step of the way.

"Arnold is transfixed by power and its uses, how to get it and how to use it," says George Butler, the force behind *Pumping Iron*. "He figured out very quickly that the road to power in America is money. His ambition knows no bounds. If you think Arnold would stop at Governor of California, you're crazy."[141]

Notes

Introduction: The Master of Reinvention

1. Joe Mathews, "So Familiar Yet So Unknown," *Los Angeles Times*, October 8, 2003, p. 1.

Chapter 1: Big Dreams in a Small Town

2. Quoted in Nancy Collins, "Pumping Arnold," *Rolling Stone*, January 17, 1985.
3. Wendy Leigh, *Arnold: An Unauthorized Biography*. Chicago: Congdon & Weed, 1990, p. 5.
4. Robert Lipsyte, *Arnold Schwarzenegger: Hercules in America*. New York: HarperCollins, 1993, p. 11.
5. Quoted in Tracy Wilkinson, "Schwarzenegger Is Still Their Hometown Hero: Residents of Thal and Graz, Austria, Remember an Athletic, Inquisitive Youth Whose Political Thinking Was Molded by a Jewish Mentor," *Los Angeles Times*, September 10, 2003.
6. Quoted in Wilkinson, "Schwarzenegger Is Still Their Hometown Hero."
7. Quoted in Leigh, *Arnold: An Unauthorized Biography*, p. 13.
8. Arnold Schwarzenegger and Douglas Kent Hall, *Arnold: The Education of a Bodybuilder*. New York: Fireside, 1977, p. 66.
9. Quoted in Terkel, *American Dreams: Lost & Found*, 1980, p. 141.
10. Quoted in Lipsyte, *Arnold Schwarzenegger: Hercules in America*, p. 6.
11. Quoted in Studs Terkel, *American Dreams: Lost & Found*. New York: Ballantine, 1980, p. 140.
12. Schwarzenegger and Hall, *Arnold: The Education of a Bodybuilder*, p. 13.
13. Schwarzenegger and Hall, *Arnold: The Education of a Bodybuilder*, p. 15.
14. Schwarzenegger and Hall, *Arnold: The Education of a Bodybuilder*, back book jacket.
15. Quoted in Leigh, *Arnold: An Unauthorized Biography*, p. 27.

16. Arnold Schwarzenegger, in the movie *Pumping Iron*, produced and directed by George Butler and Robert Fiore, 1977.

17. Schwarzenegger and Hall, *Arnold: The Education of a Bodybuilder*, p. 66.

18. Schwarzenegger and Hall, *Arnold: The Education of a Bodybuilder*, p. 19.

19. Quoted in Jack North, *Arnold Schwarzenegger*. New York: Dillon, 1995, p. 28.

20. Leigh, *Arnold: An Unauthorized Biography*, p. 29.

21. Leigh, *Arnold: An Unauthorized Biography*, p. 38.

22. Schwarzenegger and Hall, *Arnold: The Education of a Bodybuilder*, p. 38.

23. Quoted in Nigel Andrews, *True Myths: The Life and Times of Arnold Schwarzenegger*. Secaucus, NJ: Birch Lane, 1996, p. 28.

Chapter 2: The Austrian Oak

24. Schwarzenegger and Hall, *Arnold: The Education of a Bodybuilder*, p. 47.

25. Schwarzenegger and Hall, *Arnold: The Education of a Bodybuilder*, p. 40.

26. Schwarzenegger and Hall, *Arnold: The Education of a Bodybuilder*, p. 43.

27. Quoted in Andrews, *True Myths*, p. 19.

28. Schwarzenegger and Hall, *Arnold: The Education of a Bodybuilder*, p. 44.

29. Leigh, *Arnold: An Unauthorized Biography*, p. 54.

30. Quoted in Leigh, *Arnold: An Unauthorized Biography*, p. 55.

31. Schwarzenegger and Hall, *Arnold: The Education of a Bodybuilder*, p. 65.

32. Robert Lipsyte and Peter Levine, *Idols of the Game: A Sporting History of the American Century*. Atlanta, GA: Turner, 1995, p. 304.

33. Charles Gaines and George Butler, *Pumping Iron: The Art and Sport of Bodybuilding*. New York: Simon & Schuster, 1981, p. 185.

34. Gaines and Butler, *Pumping Iron*, pp. 196–97.

35. Quoted in Lipsyte, *Arnold Schwarzenegger: Hercules in America*, p. 59.

36. George Butler, *Arnold Schwarzenegger: A Portrait*. New York: Simon & Schuster, 1990, pp. 23–24.

37. Lipsyte and Levine, *Idols of the Game*, p. 307.

38. Quoted in North, *Arnold Schwarzenegger*, p. 40.

39. Quoted in Bernard Weinraub and Charlie LeDuff, "Schwarzeneg-

ger's Next Goal on Dogged, Ambitious Path," *New York Times*, August 17, 2003.

40. Lipsyte and Levine, *Idols of the Game*, p. 307.
41. Quoted in Terkel, *American Dreams*, p. 142.
42. Frank Zane, telephone interview by author, September 2003.
43. Lipsyte and Levine, *Idols of the Game*, p. 309.
44. Tom Keogh, review of *Pumping Iron* DVD, Amazon.com. www. amazon.com.
45. Schwarzenegger, in movie *Pumping Iron*.
46. Quoted in Ironage: Commemorating Bodybuilding's Glory Days, "Pumping Iron at 25: The Film That Almost Wasn't." http://ironage. us/articles/butler.html.
47. George Butler, telephone interview by author, September 2003.
48. Gaines and Butler, *Pumping Iron*, introduction.
49. Lipsyte and Levine, *Idols of the Game*, pp. 311–12.
50. Butler, *Arnold Schwarzenegger: A Portrait*, p. 21.
51. Schwarzenegger, in movie *Pumping Iron*.
52. Butler, telephone interview.
53. Butler, telephone interview.

Chapter 3: Going Hollywood

54. Quoted in Andrews, *True Myths*, p. 41.
55. Quoted in John L. Flynn, *The Films of Arnold Schwarzenegger*. New York: Citadel, 1996, p. 28.
56. Quoted in Leigh, *Arnold: An Unauthorized Biography*, p. 100.
57. Quoted in "Filmography: The Long Goodbye," Schwarzenegger. com. www.schwarzenegger.com.
58. Quoted in Flynn, *The Films of Arnold Schwarzenegger*, p. 29.
59. Quoted in David Shaw, "The World According to Arnold," *Cigar Aficionado*, Summer 1996.
60. Quoted in Joan Goodman, "Playboy Interview: Arnold Schwarzenegger," *Playboy*, January 1988.
61. Quoted in Shaw, "The World According to Arnold."
62. Quoted in "Filmography: Conan the Barbarian." Schwarzeneger.com.
63. Quoted in Collins, "Pumping Arnold," p. 52.
64. Quoted in Andrews, *True Myths*, p. 103.
65. Richard Schickel, "Overkill: Conan the Barbarian," *Time*, May 24, 1982, p. 76.
66. Jack Kroll, "A Cut-up Called Conan," *Newsweek*, May 17, 1982, p. 100.
67. Quoted in Andrews, *True Myths*, p. 108.
68. Quoted in "Filmography: The Terminator." Schwarzenegger.com.

69. Janet Maslin, *New York Times*, October 26, 1984, p. C19.
70. Janet Maslin, "In New 'Terminator,' the Forces of Good Seek Peace, Violently," *New York Times*, July 3, 1991.
71. Roger Ebert, "Terminator 2: Judgment Day," *Chicago Sun-Times*, July 3, 1991.
72. Quoted in Goodman, "Playboy Interview."
73. Roger Ebert, "Kindergarten Cop," *Chicago Sun-Times*, December 21, 1990.
74. Quoted in Jay Carr, "Schwarzenegger Inc. Hollywood's Sharpest Self-Marketer Spins a New Image," *Boston Globe*, June 18, 1993, p. 41.
75. Quoted in "Filmography: Red Sonja," Schwarzenegger.com.
76. Quoted in Shaw, "The World According to Arnold."
77. Quoted in Goodman, "Playboy Interview."
78. Quoted in Carr, "Schwarzenegger Inc.," p. 41.
79. Quoted in Dion Nissenbaum, "Arnold Schwarzenegger as . . . the Contender," *San Jose Mercury News*, August 24, 2003.
80. Stephen Hunter, "'Collateral Damage' Overshoots Its Mark," *Washington Post*, February 8, 2002, p. C01.

Chapter 4: Marrying into American Royalty

81. Quoted in Andrews, *True Myths*, p. 127.
82. Quoted in Andrews, *True Myths*, p. 81.
83. Quoted in Laurence Leamer, *The Kennedy Women: The Saga of an American Family*. New York: Villard, 1994, p. 571.
84. Maria Shriver, *Ten Things I Wish I'd Known—Before I Went Out into the Real World*. New York: Warner, 2000, p. 12.
85. Quoted in *People,* "What Makes Them Run," August 25, 2003.
86. Shriver, *Ten Things I Wish I'd Known*, p. 107.
87. Quoted in Eleanor Clift, "The Spouse: Beauty and the Barbarian," *Newsweek*, August 18, 2003.
88. Maria Shriver, on the *Oprah Winfrey Show*, ABC, September 15, 2003.
89. Maria Shriver, speech to the Commonwealth Club, Join Arnold. www.womenjoiningarnold.com/video.html.
90. Jean Mari Laskas, "The Amazing Ahhnold!" *Esquire*, July 2003, p. 68.
91. Quoted in Shaw, "The World According to Arnold."
92. Quoted in Andrews, *True Myths*, p. 79.
93. Shriver, *Ten Things I Wish I'd Known*, p. 95.
94. Arnold Schwarzenegger, "The Education of an American," transcript of speech delivered in Sacramento, California, September 21, 2001. www.schwarzenegger.com.

95. Schwarzenegger, "The Education of an American."
96. Quoted in Andrews, *True Myths*, p. 128.
97. Michael Kilian, "Shriver Weds in a Ceremony Fit for Camelot," *Chicago Tribune*, April 27, 1986, p. C1.
98. Kilian, "Shriver Weds in a Ceremony Fit for Camelot."
99. Quoted in *People*, "A Hyannis Hitching," May 12, 1986.
100. Quoted in *Los Angeles Times*, "The Recall Campaign: Recall Notebook: Registration Boosts Ranks of Voters to 2002 Levels," September 26, 2003.
101. Quoted in Shaw, "The World According to Arnold."
102. Shriver, on the *Oprah Winfrey Show*.
103. Quoted in Cynthia Hubert, "Schwarzenegger Shields His Kids," *Sacramento Bee*, October 12, 2003.
104. Shriver, on the *Oprah Winfrey Show*.
105. Quoted in Laura Mecoy, "Schwarzenegger Is Driven to Succeed," *Sacramento Bee*, September 21, 2003.
106. Quoted in Andrews, *True Myths*, p. 80.
107. Quoted in Schwarzenegger, "The Education of an American."
108. Quoted in Join Arnold, "Proposition 49." www.joinarnold.com.
109. *Sacramento Bee*, "Hasta la Vista, Prop. 49," October 3, 2002.
110. Mark Z. Barabak, "Run, Arnold, Run: The Muscleman-Turned-Actor Wants to Make the Leap into Politics. But the Hollywood Press Never Played Hardball. How Strong Is He Really?" *Los Angeles Times*, May 12, 2002.

Chapter 5: Governor Schwarzenegger

111. Quoted in Charlie LeDuff, "The Governor-Elect: Seizing the Moment, and Defying Expectations," *New York Times*, October 9, 2003, p. A23.
112. Dan Walters, "Schwarzenegger Writes New Textbooks in Focused Drive to Victory," *Sacramento Bee*, October 12, 2003.
113. California Secretary of State Official Voter Information Guide, California Statewide Special Election.
114. John Pitney, telephone interview by author, September 2003.
115. Mark Baldassare, telephone interview by author, September 2003.
116. Quoted in Hero Builders.com, "The Governor." www.herobuilders.com/orheracfig.html.
117. Quoted in Ronald Brownstein, "Washington Outlook: No Matter Who Wins, Californians Can Expect More Turmoil," *Los Angeles Times*, October 6, 2003.

118. *Los Angeles Times*, "Recall Notebook: Schwarzenegger Staff Pledges Confidentiality," September 19, 2003.
119. Richard Blow, "Full Disclosure on Full Disclosure," *New York Times*, September 27, 2003, p. A15.
120. Arnold Schwarzenegger, Join Arnold. www.joinarnold.com.
121. Joe Mathews, "The Recall Election: After a Shaky Opening, a Candidate Is Born," *Los Angeles Times*, October 9, 2003, p. A30.
122. Quoted in David Shaw, "Media Matters: A Dominant Candidate Dominated Press Coverage," *Los Angeles Times*, October 12, 2003.
123. Quoted in Daniel Weintraub, "Poised Schwarzenegger Is Vague on Fiscal Details," *Sacramento Bee*, August 21, 2003.
124. Shriver, on the *Oprah Winfrey Show*.
125. Quoted in CNN.com, "Schwarzenegger Has 'No Memory' of Lewd 1977 Interview," August 28, 2003. www.cnn.com.
126. Quoted in Erica Werner, Associated Press, September 3, 2003.
127. George Skelton, "Davis Falls Flat, While Schwarzenegger Connects," *Los Angeles Times*, August 21, 2003, p. B8.
128. Shaw, "Media Matters."
129. Quoted in Political Humor. http://politicalhumor.about.com.
130. Quoted in Mathews, "The Recall Election," p. A31.
131. LeDuff, "The Governor-Elect," p. A23.
132. Quoted in Jessica Guynn, "Republican in the Lead Spells It Out," *Contra Costa (California) Times*, October 2, 2003.
133. Quoted in *USA Today*, "Text of Arnold Schwarzenegger Apology," October 2, 2003. www.usatoday.com.
134. Quoted in Adam Nagourney and Jim Rutenberg, "Recall Race's No Longer 'Secret' Weapon," *New York Times*, October 9, 2003, p. A23.
135. John S. Caroll, "The Story Behind the Story: How the Times Decided to Publish the Accounts of 16 Women Who Said They Had Been Sexually Mistreated and Humiliated by Arnold Schwarzenegger," *Los Angeles Times*, October 12, 2003.
136. Quoted in victory speech transcript, Schwarzenegger.com. www.schwarzenegger.com.
137. Quoted in victory speech transcript, Schwarzenegger.com. www.schwarzenegger.com.
138. Kevin Starr, telephone interview by author, September 2003.
139. Starr, telephone interview by author.
140. Quoted in Roger Simon, "Does Arnold Matter?" *U.S. News & World Report*, October 20, 2003.
141. Butler, telephone interview by author.

Important Dates in the Life of Arnold Schwarzenegger

1947

Arnold Alois Schwarzenegger born July 30 in Thal, Austria.

1965

Schwarzenegger goes AWOL (absent without leave) from the Austrian military to compete in—and win—first bodybuilding contest, Mr. Europe Junior.

1966

Places second in Mr. Universe contest in London.

1967

At age twenty he becomes the youngest Mr. Universe in history.

1968

Schwarzenegger moves to the United States; loses Mr. Olympia contest to Frank Zane.

1970

Wins first of seven Mr. Olympia contests; makes inauspicious movie debut as Hercules.

1974

Schwarzenegger is featured in the book, *Pumping Iron.*

1975

He announces retirement from bodybuilding.

1976

He wins Golden Globe for Best New Male Star of the Year for role in *Stay Hungry.*

1977
Schwarzenegger stars in documentary film *Pumping Iron*; publishes his best-selling autobiography and bodybuilding guide.

1980
Stages surprise return to bodybuilding, winning Mr. Olympia title for a then-unprecedented seventh time.

1982
Stars in *Conan the Barbarian.*

1983
Becomes a U.S. citizen.

1984
Stars in *Conan the Destroyer* and *The Terminator.*

1986
Schwarzenegger weds Maria Shriver.

1988
He appears in first comedy, *Twins.*

1989
Daughter Katherine is born.

1990
President George H.W. Bush names Schwarzenegger chairman of the President's Council on Physical Fitness and Sports.

1991
Schwarzenegger stars in *Terminator 2*; daughter Christina is born; he establishes the charitable organization, Inner-City Games.

1993
Son Patrick is born.

1997
Son Christopher is born.

2002
Schwarzenegger heads successful campaign for Proposition 49, a California ballot measure intending to expand before-and-after-school care for children.

2003
Stars in *Terminator 3*; enters and wins first election to public office, becoming governor of California.

For Further Reading

Books

David L. Chapman, *Sandow the Magnificent: Eugen Sandow and the Beginnings of Bodybuilding (Sport and Society)*. Champaign: University of Illinois Press, 1994. The story of the first bodybuilding showman, whom many consider the father of the bodybuilding business, with extensive photos. One reviewer said, "Arnold, eat your heart out!"

Arnold Schwarzenegger, *Arnold's Bodybuilding for Men*. New York: Simon & Schuster, 1984. Advice book for male bodybuilders, with a special section aimed at teenagers.

———, *Arnold's Bodyshaping for Women*. New York: Simon & Schuster, 1979. Schwarzenegger's fitness advice tailored for women.

———, *The New Encyclopedia of Modern Bodybuilding: The Bible of Bodybuilding, Fully Updated and Revised*. New York: Simon & Schuster, 1999. Detailed and lengthy (832 pages) book that is literally considered the bible of bodybuilding, with Schwarzenegger's tips on training and eating, bodybuilding lore and history, and extensive photos.

Arnold Schwarzenegger and Charles Gaines, *Arnold's Fitness for Kids Ages Birth–5: A Guide to Health, Exercise, and Nutrition*. New York: Doubleday, 1993. A book that provides sound advice for parents about how to help their children to become fit and healthy.

Darrell M. West and John M. Orman, *Celebrity Politics*. White
Plains, NY: Prentice-Hall, 2002. A book that examines the
evolution and impact of celebrity politics in the United States.

Websites

Golden Raspberry Award Foundation (www.razzies.com). A
website chronicling the "winners" of the Razzies, "honoring"
the worst feats in moviemaking.

Hero Builders (www.herobuilders.com). A website that sells
action-figure dolls based on real-life heroes and villains and
other figures in the news.

The Internet Movie Database (http://us.imdb.com). Includes
incredible details about movies, movie stars, and awards.

Sandow: Historic Photographs of Early Bodybuilders
(www.sandowmuseum.com). Pays homage to Eugen Sandow
and other early bodybuilders with historical information and
photos.

Works Consulted

Books

Nigel Andrews, *True Myths: The Life and Times of Arnold Schwarzenegger.* Secaucus, NJ: Birch Lane, 1996. Detailed biography by a British film critic focusing on how much of Schwarzenegger's storied life is myth and how much is real.

George Butler, *Arnold Schwarzenegger: A Portrait.* New York: Simon & Schuster, 1990. An unusual and vivid portrait in words and photos of Schwarzenegger during his bodybuilding career.

John L. Flynn, *The Films of Arnold Schwarzenegger.* New York: Citadel, 1996. A book that offers flattering descriptions of Schwarzenegger's films and details of how they were made.

Charles Gaines and George Butler, *Pumping Iron: The Art and Sport of Bodybuilding.* New York: Simon & Schuster, 1981. Beautifully photographed and evocatively written book chronicling the sport of bodybuilding, its history, and best-known practitioners.

Laurence Leamer, *The Kennedy Women: The Saga of an American Family.* New York: Villard, 1994. Bible-thick tale of generations of Kennedys, focusing on the females.

Wendy Leigh, *Arnold: An Unauthorized Biography.* Chicago: Congdon & Weed, 1990. A detailed biography produced in the face of extraordinary opposition from Schwarzenegger because of unflattering subjects it raises.

Robert Lipsyte, *Arnold Schwarzenegger: Hercules in America.* New York: HarperCollins, 1993. A pithy book about Schwarzenegger by a former prizewinning sportswriter for the *New York Times* that puts the superstar's achievements in the context of the day.

Robert Lipsyte and Peter Levine, *Idols of the Game: A Sporting History of the American Century.* Atlanta, GA: Turner, 1995. A book of provocative profiles of sixteen sports idols, offering a sophisticated analysis of how the sporting stars reflected the tenor of the times in which they played.

Jack North, *Arnold Schwarzenegger*. New York: Dillon, 1995. A laudatory account of Schwarzenegger's life.

Arnold Schwarzenegger and Douglas Kent Hall, *Arnold: The Education of a Bodybuilder*. New York: Fireside, 1977. The best-selling and fascinating first-person account of Schwarzenegger's bodybuilding career and bodybuilding training recommendations.

Maria Shriver, *Ten Things I Wish I'd Known—Before I Went Out into the Real World*. New York: Warner, 2000. A graduation-gift-style advice book modeled on a commencement ceremony speech Shriver gave about her insights on life's lessons learned.

Studs Terkel, *American Dreams: Lost & Found*. New York: Ballantine, 1980. The best-selling compendium of a hundred Americans' reflections on their lives and what it means to be an American.

Susan Zannos, *Arnold Schwarzenegger*. Bear, DE: Mitchell Lane, 2000. Very short and simplistic children's account of Schwarzenegger's life.

Periodicals

Mark Z. Barabak, "Run, Arnold, Run: The Muscleman-Turned-Actor Wants to Make the Leap into Politics. But the Hollywood Press Never Played Hardball. How Strong Is He Really?" *Los Angeles Times*, May 12, 2002.

Richard Blow, "Full Disclosure on Full Disclosure," *New York Times*, September 27, 2003.

Ronald Brownstein, "Washington Outlook: No Matter Who Wins, Californians Can Expect More Turmoil," *Los Angeles Times*, October 6, 2003.

Jay Carr, "Schwarzenegger Inc. Hollywood's Sharpest Self-Marketer Spins a New Image," *Boston Globe*, June 18, 1993.

John S. Carroll, "The Story Behind the Story: How the Times Decided to Publish the Accounts of 16 Women Who Said They Had Been Sexually Mistreated and Humiliated by Arnold Schwarzenegger," *Los Angeles Times*, October 12, 2003.

Eleanor Clift, "The Spouse: Beauty and the Barbarian," *Newsweek*, August 18, 2003.

Nancy Collins, "Pumping Arnold," *Rolling Stone*, January 17, 1985.

Roger Ebert, "Kindergarten Cop," *Chicago Sun-Times*, December 21, 1990.

———, "Terminator 2: Judgment Day," *Chicago Sun-Times*, July 3, 1991.

Joan Goodman, "Playboy Interview: Arnold Schwarzenegger," *Playboy*, January 1988.

Jessica Guynn, "Republican in the Lead Spells It Out," *Contra Costa (California) Times*, October 2, 2003.

Vicki Haddock, "President Schwarzenegger? Some Think It's Time to Stop Excluding Foreign-Born Citizens from Serving in the Oval Office," *San Francisco Chronicle*, November 2, 2003.

Cynthia Hubert, "Schwarzenegger Shields His Kids," *Sacramento Bee*, October 12, 2003.

Stephen Hunter, "'Collateral Damage' Overshoots Its Mark," *Washington Post*, February 8, 2002.

Michael Kilian, "Shriver Weds in a Ceremony Fit for Camelot," *Chicago Tribune*, April 27, 1986.

Jack Kroll, "A Cut-up Called Conan," *Newsweek*, May 17, 1982.

Jean Mari Laskas, "The Amazing Ahhnold!" *Esquire*, July 2003.

Charlie LeDuff, "The Governor-Elect: Seizing the Moment, and Defying Expectations," *New York Times*, October 9, 2003.

Susanna Loof, "Records Show Schwarzenegger's Father Was a Nazi Storm Trooper," Associated Press, *Sacramento Bee*, August 24, 2003.

Los Angeles Times, "The Recall Campaign: Recall Notebook: Registration Boosts Ranks of Voters to 2002 Levels," September 26, 2003.

———, "Recall Notebook: Schwarzenegger Staff Pledges Confidentiality," September 19, 2003.

Peter Manso, "Conversation with Arnold Schwarzenegger: The Man with the World's Most Perfectly Developed Physique Destroys a Few Myths About Bodybuilding: He Smokes Dope, Stays Out Late and Forgets to Take His Vitamins," *Oui*, August 1977.

Janet Maslin, "In New 'Terminator,' the Forces of Good Seek Peace, Violently," *New York Times*, July 3, 1991.

———, *New York Times*, October 26, 1984.

Joe Mathews, "The Recall Election: After a Shaky Opening, a Candidate Is Born," *Los Angeles Times*, October 9, 2003.

———, "So Familiar Yet So Unknown," *Los Angeles Times*, October 8, 2003.

Laura Mecoy, "Schwarzenegger Is Driven to Succeed," *Sacramento Bee*, September 21, 2003.

Adam Nagourney and Jim Rutenberg, "Recall Race's No Longer 'Secret' Weapon," *New York Times*, October 9, 2003.

Dion Nissenbaum, "Arnold Schwarzenegger as . . . the Contender," *San Jose Mercury News*, August 24, 2003.

People, "A Hyannis Hitching," May 12, 1986.

———, "What Makes Them Run," August 25, 2003.

Sacramento Bee, "Hasta la Vista, Prop. 49," October 3, 2002.

Richard Schickel, "Overkill: Conan the Barbarian," *Time*, May 24, 1982.

David Shaw, "Media Matters: A Dominant Candidate Dominated Press Coverage," *Los Angeles Times*, October 12, 2003.

————, "The World According to Arnold," *Cigar Aficionado*, Summer 1996.

Roger Simon, "Does Arnold Matter?" *U.S. News & World Report*, October 20, 2003.

George Skelton, "Davis Falls Flat, While Schwarzenegger Connects," *Los Angeles Times*, August 21, 2003.

Dan Walters, "Schwarzenegger Writes New Textbooks in Focused Drive to Victory," *Sacramento Bee*, October 12, 2003.

Bernard Weinraub and Charlie LeDuff, "Schwarzenegger's Next Goal on Dogged, Ambitious Path," *New York Times*, August 17, 2003.

Daniel Weintraub, "Poised Schwarzenegger Is Vague on Fiscal Details," *Sacramento Bee*, August 21, 2003.

Erica Werner, Associated Press, September 3, 2003.

Tracy Wilkinson, "Schwarzenegger Is Still Their Hometown Hero: Residents of Thal and Graz, Austria, Remember an Athletic, Inquisitive Youth Whose Political Thinking Was Molded by a Jewish Mentor," *Los Angeles Times*, September 10, 2003.

Internet Sources

California Secretary of State Official Voter Information Guide, California Statewide Special Election, October 7, 2003. http://www.voter guide.ss.ca.gov/english.pdf.

CBSNEWS.com, "FDA: Designer Steroid Illegal." www.cbsnews.com.

CNN.com, "Schwarzenegger Has 'No Memory' of Lewd 1977 Interview," August 28, 2003. www.cnn.com.

Current Comment from the American College of Sports Medicine, "Anabolic Steroids." www.acsm.org.

"Cutting Teens' Steroid Use." www.healthatoz.com.

E! Online, Arnold Schwarzenegger fact sheet. www.eonline.com.

Filmography. "The Long Goodbye." Schwarzenegger.com. www.schwar zenegger.com.

Monika Guttman, "Schwarzenegger Gets New Role: Patient at University Hospital." USC press release. www.usc.edu.

Hero Builders.com, "The Governator." www.herobuilders.com/orher acfig.html.

InfoFacts, Steroids, National Institute on Drug Abuse. http://165.112. 78.61/Infofact/steroids.html.

Ironage: Commemorating Bodybuilding's Glory Days, "Pumping Iron at 25: The Film That Almost Wasn't." http://ironage.us/articles/butler.html.

Join Arnold, "Proposition 49." www.joinarnold.com.

Tom Keogh, review of *Pumping Iron* DVD, Amazon.com. www.amazon.com.

Arnold Schwarzenegger, "The Education of an American," transcript of speech delivered in Sacramento, California, September 21, 2001. www.schwarzenegger.com.

Maria Shriver, speech to Commonwealth Club, Join Arnold. www.womenjoiningarnold.com/video.html.

USA Today, "Text of Arnold Schwarzenegger Apology," October 2, 2003. www.USAToday.com.

U.S. Food and Drug Administration, "FDA Statement on THG." www.fda.gov.

Movies and Television

Oprah Winfrey Show, ABC, September 15, 2003.

Pumping Iron, movie produced and directed by George Butler and Robert Fiore, 1977.

Websites

CNN.com (www.cnn.com). The website of the twenty-four-hour news television station.

Political Humor (http://politicalhumor.about.com). A website chronicling political humor from a wide variety of sources.

Rotten Tomatoes (www.rottentomatoes.com). A highly praised website offering all manner of reviews and information about movies.

Schwarzenneger.com (www.schwarzenegger.com). Schwarzenegger's Internet site, showcasing his bodybuilding, film, and political careers, his charitable causes, and his merchandise.

Index

Picture Credits

About the Author

Karen Brandon is an award-winning journalist who lives in Leucadia, California, with her husband, son, and daughter—the people who pump (clap!) her up.